Developments in Health Economics and Public Policy

Volume 14

This series publishes recent economic research and its applications to public policy problems of health and health services. Topics of interest include the production and measurement of health or health status; economic evaluation of appropriate therapies; production of health services; price, financing, supply and demand for health services; competition and monopoly in health services and insurance markets; information and health care markets; adverse selection in health services and insurance markets; regulations and planning of health services; nonprice rationing; occupational licensure and regulation; the political economy of health policy. Though the economic or policy problem motivating an analysis may be country-specific, the books will be of interest to an international audience. Aside from a core group of specialists in health economics, the books will be accessible to general non-specialist economists and to non-economists in related areas, such as health policy, epidemiology or public health.

All titles in the series are peer-reviewed.

Pierre Pestieau

The Economics of Long-term Care

The Contribution of Family, State and Market to Elder Care

Springer

Pierre Pestieau
University of Liege
Liege, Belgium

ISSN 0927-4987
Developments in Health Economics and Public Policy
ISBN 978-3-032-18236-4   ISBN 978-3-032-18237-1 (eBook)
https://doi.org/10.1007/978-3-032-18237-1

This Springer imprint is published by the registered company Springer Nature Switzerland AG
The registered company address is: Gewerbestrasse 11, 6330 Cham, Switzerland

Acknowledgements

I gratefully acknowledge the financial support of the Chaire "Marché des risques et création de valeur" of the FdR/SCOR. I am also deeply indebted to my coauthors, whose collaborations on research related to aging and long-term care over the past two decades have been both rewarding and inspiring. Finally, I extend my sincere thanks to three anonymous referees for their insightful comments and constructive suggestions.

Contents

List of Figures

List of Tables

Chapter 1
Introduction

The aging of populations worldwide has significant implications for the provision of old-age long-term care (LTC).[1] As the proportion of elderly individuals increases, several key areas are particularly affected. First of all, there is an increased demand for LTC services. An aging population leads to a higher prevalence of age-related health conditions such as dementia, arthritis, and mobility issues, which in turn increases the demand for long-term care services. This includes both in-home care services and residential care facilities.

Secondly, the demand for healthcare professionals, including nurses, caregivers, and support staff specializing in geriatric care, is expected to rise. There might be shortages in the workforce if fewer younger people are available to replace retiring workers or to meet increasing demands. A solution may rest on technological innovations. There may be a push toward more technological solutions to help manage the care of older adults more efficiently. Innovations like telemedicine, remote monitoring, and assistive technologies could play significant roles in addressing the growing need while also potentially reducing costs.

Thirdly, with more people requiring long-term care, there will likely be increased financial pressure on both public and private healthcare systems. Funding these services through insurance, out-of-pocket payments, or tax-funded systems could require new financial strategies or reforms. Governments and organizations may need to develop and adapt policies that support the aging population. This could involve changes in housing policies, the development of age-friendly communities, and increased support for family caregivers.

Fourthly, the family that has been the main provider of LTC services may have to adapt in this new setting where the ratio of those demanding needs to those able to fulfill them is increasing. The social fabric of communities may also change. There

[1] This book focuses specifically on long-term care services for older adults. It does not address the substantial population of children and adults who require long-term care for mental and physical health reasons.

P. Pestieau, *The Economics of Long-term Care*, Developments in Health Economics and Public Policy 14, https://doi.org/10.1007/978-3-032-18237-1_1

could be a greater need for community-based programs and services that support not only the physical health of older adults but also their mental and social well-being.

Addressing the implications of an aging population on long-term care will require comprehensive strategies that integrate the market, the state and the family to ensure that the needs of older adults are met effectively and compassionately. Each plays a distinct and crucial role, often complementing each other to ensure that the needs of elderly individuals are met effectively.[2]

The state[3] plays a foundational role in the provision of long-term care through regulation, funding, and direct service provision. The state provides financial support for care through programs such as Medicaid in the U.S., or national health services in most countries. This can help cover costs of nursing homes, home health care, and other necessary services. In some cases, the government may also provide care services directly through public nursing home or implement policies that support family caregivers, such as tax benefits or paid leave policies. Another important mission of the state is to establish standards and regulations to ensure the quality and safety of care. Avoiding abuse both in institutions or at home is increasingly necessary.

Families often provide a significant portion, indeed the most important, of long-term care, either directly or by arranging and supervising care. Their role includes direct caregiving and emotional support. Many families take on the role of caregivers, providing daily assistance with activities such as bathing, feeding, and medication management. Beyond physical care, families contribute to the emotional well-being of their elderly members by maintaining close relationships and social connections.

Private sector involvement is crucial, especially where state and family provisions are inadequate. The market's role includes private insurance, offering long-term care package that helps cover the costs of care that state programs might not fully cover. It also provides private care through nursing homes, assisted living facilities, and home health care services. One also has to rely on the market for innovation and development. The private sector drives innovation in eldercare, including the development of new technologies and care models that can improve the quality and efficiency of care.

The interaction between the state, the family, and the market can vary greatly depending on the country's social policies, cultural norms, and economic conditions. Challenges in this system can include significant disparities in the availability and quality of care based on geographic, economic, and social factors. Financial resources, family altruism, and severity of the disability vary quite a lot from one elderly to another. In sum, a balanced approach that leverages the strengths of the state, the family, and the market, while addressing their limitations, is crucial for providing comprehensive and humane care to the elderly. This balance is dynamic and requires ongoing adjustments to respond to demographic changes and advances in healthcare.

---

[2] For earlier and shorter surveys, see Norton (2016) and Klimaviciute and Pestieau (2018, 2023).

[3] State here refers to the government.

In this work, we challenge certain commonly held beliefs, particularly the notion that family support is always altruistic and benevolent. We will indicate that much of the care provided by family members, including children and spouses, is rooted not in altruism but in familial and cultural norms. More critically, we will address the issue of mistreatment, which can be institutional but also familial. Such behaviors are especially harmful because the victims are often in a state of extreme vulnerability.

This book focuses specifically on OECD member countries, with particular emphasis on European societies. The evidence presented draws primarily from SHARE (Survey of Health, Ageing and Retirement in Europe), which provides comprehensive data on aging populations across the continent. It is structured as follows. After an introductory chapter, Chapter 2 examines aging and disability in old age, both across countries and over time. Chapter 3 focuses on the key institutions responsible for long-term care: the state, the market, and the family. It explores why the insurance market remains almost invisible and why care provided by children and spouses is becoming increasingly unreliable. While the book is largely non-technical, Chapter 4 introduces several analytical models that illustrate how the State could address long-term care needs in conjunction with the market, when available, and the family. Chapter 5 tackles two particularly sensitive topics: elder abuse and end-of-life care. The book concludes with a final chapter summarizing key insights.

References

Klimaviciute, J. & Pestieau, P. (2018). The public economics of long-term care. A survey of recent contributions. *Annals of Public and Cooperative Economics, 89* (1), 49–64.

Klimaviciute, J. & Pestieau, P. (2023). The economics of long-term care. An overview, *The Journal of Economic Surveys, 37*, 1192–1213.

Norton, E. (2016). Health and long-term care. In *Handbook of the economics of population aging*, 1, chapter 16 (pp. 951–989).

Chapter 2
Some Evidence

2.1 Increasing Demand for LTC

The demand for long-term care in advanced countries is rising, driven by demographic shifts, including aging populations, increasing life expectancy, and changes in family structures. We now present evidence supporting this trend.

2.1.1 Aging Population

The old-age dependency[1] ratio in OECD countries has risen significantly over the past 70 years and is expected to continue increasing in the coming decades. As a reminder, old-age dependency ratio is the number of individuals aged 65 or older per 100 people of working age, defined as those aged between 20 and 64 years old. Projections are drawn from the United Nations, World Population Prospects 2022. Table 2.1 presents some evidence for a sample of countries, the European Union (EU) and the OECD.

Currently, there are 31 individuals aged 65 and over for every 100 people of working age (20–64) on average across these OECD countries, compared to only 20 thirty years ago and 14 seventy years ago. The trend of population aging is accelerating, as this ratio—calculated with constant age thresholds—is projected to reach 66 within the next 70 years. However, the progression of old-age dependency ratios varies substantially across countries. Japan, the demographically oldest OECD country, currently has an old-age dependency ratio of 55.4%. Finland and Italy also have elevated ratios, both exceeding 40%. By 2052, Greece (70.7%), Italy (78.1%),

[1] Old age dependency has two different meanings. Either it refers to the ratio of elderly people (typically those aged 65 and over) to the working-age population (usually defined as ages 15–64) or, in the context of disability, it refers to the loss of functional independence that can occur as people age, resulting in the need for assistance with daily activities and self-care.

P. Pestieau, *The Economics of Long-term Care*, Developments in Health Economics and Public Policy 14, https://doi.org/10.1007/978-3-032-18237-1_2

Table 2.1 Old age dependency ratios

	1952	1992	2022	2082
France	19.7	24.9	39.3	68.4
Germany	16.9	23.7	36.0	^64.8
Italy	14.8	25.4	41.0	83.4
Spain	13.0	24.3	33.4	84.7
Japan	9.9	21.6	55.4	85.7
UK	18.3	26.9	33.2	63.6
USA	14.9	21.0	29.4	58.7
OECD	13.8	20.4	31.3	66.1
EU27*	14.8	22.3	34.6	66.7

OECD (2023a)
*EU27 refers to the 27 European Union member states after the UK left the EU.

Table 2.2 Fertility rates

	1962	1982	2022	2062
France	2.77	1.92	1.70	1.76
Germany	2.50	1.49	1.59	1.59
Italy	2.40	1.56	1.29	1.47
Spain	2,70	1.93	1.29	1.47
Japan	1.99	1.70	1.31	1.50
UK	2.89	1.77	1.57	1.66
USA	3.34	1.82	1.66	1.70
OECD	3.30	2.15	1.59	1.63
EU27	2.50	1.93	1.53	1.62

OECD (2023a)

Japan (80.0%), Korea (82.3%), and Spain (77.2%) are expected to see their ratios surpass 70%. In fact, by 2082, Korea's ratio could reach an extraordinary 117%.

While the rise in the population aged 65 and over has been notable across OECD countries, the growth has been particularly sharp among the oldest cohort—those aged 80 and above. By 2050, the share of people aged 80 and older is projected to more than double on average in OECD countries. In nearly half (17) of OECD countries, at least 1 in 10 people will be 80 or older by 2050. In six countries—Lithuania, Portugal, Italy, Greece, Korea, and Japan—more than one in eight will be 80 or older. This demographic shift is particularly significant as long-term care needs are most pronounced among those aged 80 and above.

Declining fertility and increased longevity explain these trends. As it appears on Table 2.2, fertility rates currently average 1.59 across OECD countries, well below the level that ensures population replacement. The trend to fewer children started in the late 1950s. The average fertility rate across OECD countries has stabilized close to 1.6 over the last two decades and is projected to remain at this level in the

Table 2.3 Life expectancy at age 65 in 2022 and 2065

	Women		Men		Difference*	
	2022	2065	2022	2065	2022	2065
France	88.7	92.6	85.0	89.0	3.7	3.6
Germany	86.2	90.9	82.9	88.4	3.4	2.5
Italy	88.0	92.2	85.0	99.2	3.0	3.0
Spain	88.6	92.7	84.7	88.8	3.8	3.9
Japan	89.9	94.1	85.1	89.1	4.8	5.0
UK	86.7	90.2	84.5	87.4	2.2	2.8
USA	88.9	90.1	83.1	88.4	2.8	1.7
OECD	86.2	90.6	83.0	87.9	3.2	2.7
EU27	85.6	90.2	82.2	87.4	3.4	2.8

OECD (2023a)
*Difference between life expectancy of women and men

future. In the EU, the fertility rate is even lower with 1.53 in 2022. Here also there is a large variety of situations with 1.80 in France and 1.30 in Spain and Italy. The lowest fertility is in Korea with a rate of 0.87.

The remarkable increase in life expectancy is one of the greatest achievements of the last century. Lives continue to get longer, and this trend is predicted to continue although the pace of improvement in old age has slowed recently, and particularly given COVID-19. As shown in Table 2.3, in 2022, life expectancy at age 65 averaged 83 years for men and 86.2 years for women. The figure was highest for women in Japan (89.9 years) and men in Australia, New Zealand, and Switzerland (at 85.3 years or more) and lowest for women in Hungary and the Slovak Republic (below 83 years) and men in Lithuania (78.1 years). On average across OECD countries, remaining life expectancy at age 65 is projected to increase by 4.4 years among women and 4.9 years among men by 2065.The gender gap in life expectancy at age 65 is predicted to be between almost two and four years in favor of women in nearly all OECD countries in 2065.

Note that we here use period life expectancy figures and not cohort life expectancy. Those two concepts provide different perspectives on how long people live. Period life expectancy reflects mortality rates of a specific time period, while cohort life expectancy considers projected mortality improvements for a specific birth cohort over their lifetime. In essence, period life expectancy is a snapshot of a moment, while cohort life expectancy is a projection of a group's lifespan. Period life expectancies tend to be lower than cohort life expectancies.

Aging populations are more prone to chronic conditions leading to a more or less high loss of autonomy. In 2021, the greatest burden of disability among older people in the EU stemmed primarily from dementias—including Alzheimer's disease, Parkinson's disease, and falls. Other significant causes of healthy life years lost due to disability included diabetes, arthritis, depression and anxiety, as well as cerebrovascular and ischemic heart diseases. As the population ages, Alzheimer's disease and other dementias stand out as one of the most pressing challenges in EU countries. Despite extensive research and substantial financial investments, there is still no cure for these conditions, and existing treatments can at best slow their progression while potentially causing side effects that negatively impact quality of life. This underscores the urgent need to prioritize preventive measures.

In 2021, it was estimated that nearly 8 million people across EU countries were living with Alzheimer's disease or another form of dementia. Among individuals aged 70 and over, more than 9% were affected, with prevalence rising sharply with age—from 3% among those aged 70-74 to 18% for individuals over 80. These figures highlight the growing burden of dementia as Europe's population continues to age. Falls also pose a significant risk for older adults, often resulting in emergency department visits, hospital admissions, and long-lasting effects on mobility and quality of life. Several factors contribute to this increased risk, including a decline in muscle strength and balance, reduced physical activity, impaired vision, multiple medications, and malnutrition. Poor living conditions and inadequate home lighting further increase the likelihood of falls. According to data from the Survey of Health, Aging and Retirement in Europe (SHARE), the proportion of older people affected by falls rises markedly with age, and the gender gap becomes more apparent among the elderly. In 2021–2022, nearly one in six (16%) individuals aged 75 and older reported experiencing a fall within the previous 6 months across EU countries, with the rate being notably higher among women (18%).

2.1.2 Changing Family Structures

Declining birth rates across Europe have resulted in smaller family units. As a result, there are fewer family members available to provide informal care for the elderly. This shift is placing more pressure on formal long-term care systems. Increased urbanization and migration patterns have led to family members living further apart, making it difficult for families to care for their elderly relatives. This trend has further fueled the demand for formal LTC services. The evolution of family structures is increasingly shaped by the growing uncertainty faced by disabled parents regarding the care and support they can expect from their relatives. Various life events—such as the loss of a family member, serious illness, migration, economic struggles, or interpersonal conflicts—can unexpectedly disrupt these support systems. As a result, the reliability of family-based assistance becomes less predictable, reinforcing the need for alternative mechanisms to ensure adequate care and stability.

Death of caregivers creates an immediate and often permanent gap in support. When an adult child or spouse who provides daily assistance passes away, the disabled parent may be left without their primary caregiver and emotional support. Illness can affect both the caregiver and the disabled parent. A previously healthy family member might develop their own health issues, limiting their ability to provide care. Alternatively, the disabled parent's condition might worsen, requiring more specialized care than family members can provide. Migration for employment, education, or personal reasons can physically separate caregivers from those who need care. When adult children move to different cities or countries for better opportunities, the geographic distance makes daily assistance impossible.

Economic hardship can force family caregivers to work longer hours or take multiple jobs, reducing their availability. Financial stress might also mean families can no longer afford to subsidize the disabled parent's care needs or living arrangements. Family disputes and relationship breakdowns can sever caregiving arrangements. Disagreements about care responsibilities, inheritance issues, or longstanding family tensions might lead to the withdrawal of support from previously reliable family members. These disruptions often create cascading effects, where disabled parents must quickly find alternative care arrangements, potentially face institutional care, or struggle with unmet needs. The emotional impact can be significant as well, adding psychological stress to physical challenges.

2.1.3 *Forecasting Future Demand*

A recent European Commission study by Belmonte et al. (2023) presents a prototype microsimulation demographic model[2] projecting the risk of developing long-term care demand for the over-50 population in 19 selected European countries from 2011 to 2070. Using data from SHARE, the study indicates a persistent trend of increasing long-term care demand and chronic diseases, primarily due to demographic aging. According to the baseline scenario, the prevalence of LTC demand is expected to rise from 11.6% in 2020 to 14.1% in 2070, representing a 21% increase from 2020 levels. In absolute terms, the number of people with LTC needs in the 19 EU countries is projected to grow from 19.7 million in 2020 to 20.9 million in 2025, 27.1 million in 2050, and 28.7 million in 2070. In a scenario in which improving education levels do not translate into increased autonomy, the prevalence of LTC demand in 2070 would increase by 43% compared to 21% in the baseline scenario.

2.1.4 *Increased Public LTC*

Governments are recognizing the growing need for long-term care and are increasing their spending on LTC services. For example, the European Commission's Ageing Report (EC, 2024) projects that public spending on long-term care in the EU will increase from 1.7% of GDP in 2022 to 2.6% by 2070, reflecting the growing demand. This projection applies to the baseline scenario. This is equivalent to an increase of expenditure by 48%. The variation in the projected expenditures in % of GDP ranges from a stable overall pattern in Greece to increases above 100% in Spain and Denmark as it appears on Table 2.4. One also observes a variation in the generosity of public

[2] See also Marois and Aktas (2021).

Table 2.4 Public expenditures on LTC (% of GDP 2022–2070)

	2022	2070	% change
France	1.9	2.6	38
Germany	1.9	2.3	25
Italy	1.6	2.1	31
Spain	0.8	1.7	108
Denmark	3.0	6.2	109
Netherlands	3.8	5.7	48
EU27	1.7	2.6	47

EC (2024)

programs. The Netherlands devote 3.8 % of their GDP to LTC whereas Spain devotes only 0.8%.

In an interesting paper, Costa-font et al. (2015) examine the financing of LTC, distinguishing between ex ante (before the need arises) and ex post (after the need arises) mechanisms. The study suggests that ex ante and ex post mechanisms are largely substitutes, meaning that the extent to which one is used can influence the need for the other. Additionally, it appears that public LTC spending is significantly affected by a country's income, the proportion of elderly citizens, and the extent of informal care.

2.1.5 LTC Workforce Shortage

The increasing demand for long-term care services is also leading to workforce shortage in the LTC sector. This subsection focuses on paid caretakers, not unpaid caregivers such as family members, who may also be unavailable for reasons discussed above. The shortage of caretakers in nursing homes is a complex issue stemming from several interrelated factors. Understanding these causes and exploring potential solutions can help address the problem effectively. There are several factors explaining this shortage. the main ones are low wages and benefits, high physical and emotional demands, lack of training and advancement opportunities, and public perception. Caretaker roles are often low-paying, with limited benefits. This discourages individuals from pursuing or staying in these positions. The work is physically taxing, emotionally challenging, and sometimes involves irregular hours. These factors lead to burnout and high turnover rates. Limited access to training programs and career progression makes the role less attractive to potential employees. Finally, caretaking is often undervalued in society, which can deter people from entering the field. To address the shortage of caregivers, several comprehensive solutions can be implemented. Offering competitive salaries and comprehensive benefits packages is a critical step toward attracting and retaining workers in the caregiving sector.

In addition, providing hazard pay or bonuses for roles involving significant challenges can serve as an effective incentive. Improving working conditions is equally essential, which can be achieved by establishing manageable caregiver-to-patient ratios to alleviate excessive workloads and by investing in supportive technologies designed to streamline caregiving tasks. Furthermore, ensuring the accessibility and affordability of training programs, including certifications and on-the-job learning opportunities, is crucial for equipping caregivers with the necessary skills. Clear pathways for professional growth, such as progression into nursing or management roles, should also be developed to enhance career prospects within the field. In many countries, caregiving is predominantly undertaken by immigrants, a trend that is expected to persist due to declining fertility rates. This demographic reality underscores the need for policies that support and integrate immigrant caregivers into the workforce effectively. Finally, public awareness initiatives play a vital role in addressing the caregiver shortage.

Promoting the importance of caregiving through targeted campaigns and community programs can help elevate the profession's reputation and encourage broader participation. Collectively, these strategies form a multifaceted approach to resolving the challenges associated with the caregiving workforce shortage. As it is clear, addressing the caretaker shortage requires a multifaceted approach involving increased investment, societal change, and policy reform. By improving conditions, offering incentives, and leveraging technology, we can make caregiving a sustainable and rewarding career. In Europe, the shortage of carers in the long-term care sector has become a pressing issue due to the decline in the workforce available for such roles. One clearly would need a real political will to face those problems.

Migrant care workers are increasingly seen as a potential solution to this challenge. Their involvement in the sector addresses a critical gap, as many European countries struggle to meet the rising demand for long-term care services. Migrant workers bring a unique value to the care industry, as they often possess the skills and willingness to take on roles that are sometimes viewed as less desirable by local workers. These jobs are often characterized by long hours, demanding physical and emotional responsibilities, and comparatively low wages. For many migrants, however, such roles offer an entry point into the labor market, providing financial stability and opportunities to integrate into their host societies. While the potential for migrant workers to mitigate the care crisis is evident, their integration into the workforce is not without challenges. Legal and administrative barriers, such as restrictive immigration policies and lengthy work visa processes, can hinder the recruitment of qualified caregivers from abroad. Cultural and language barriers also may also play a significant role. At the same time, these differences can sometimes be an advantage.

Migrant workers from southern regions bring distinctive cultural strengths to elder care, particularly their deep-rooted traditions of patience and empathy toward older adults. These values stem from societies where reverence for elders remains central to social fabric—a stark contrast to many Western contexts where aging populations face increasing marginalization amid youth-oriented cultural priorities. This cultural alignment positions migrant care workers as a vital resource for addressing Europe's mounting long-term care crisis. However, realizing this potential demands comprehensive integration strategies that harmonize the needs of care workers, elderly recipients, and the communities they serve. Success will require policies that recognize both the unique contributions these workers bring and the structural support necessary for sustainable, dignified care systems. With the right measures in place, they can play a crucial role in alleviating the care shortage while enriching the cultural and social fabric of their host communities.

2.2 Disability-Free Life Expectancy

To assess the growth of LTC needs, a natural measure is the disability-free life expectancy (or "healthy life-years"), which is defined as the number of years spent free of activity limitation. In Europe, this indicator is calculated annually by Eurostat for European countries.[3] The disability measure is based on the global activity limitation indicator (GALI) question in the EU-SILC survey: "For at least the past 6 months, have you been hampered because of a health problem in activities people usually do? Yes, strongly limited / yes, limited / no, not limited."In the EU, the number of healthy life years at birth in 2022 was 62.8 years for women and 62.4 years for men, a gender gap of 0.4 years. Life expectancy in 2022 was 83.3 years for women and 77.9 years for men, a gap of 5.4 years. As the gender gap was considerably smaller in terms of healthy life years than it was for overall life expectancy, most of the additional years of life expectancy for women tend to be lived with activity limitations. Therefore, men tended to spend a greater share (80.1%) of their somewhat shorter lives free from activity limitations than women (75.4%).

Across the EU countries, life expectancy at birth for women in 2022 ranged between 77.9 years in Bulgaria and 85.9 years in Spain; a difference of 8.0 years. A similar comparison for men shows that the lowest life expectancy in 2022 was recorded in Latvia at 69.4 years and the highest in Sweden 81.4 years; a range of 12.0 years.

As such, there were considerably wider differences between EU countries in terms of healthy years, when compared with the overall differences in life expectancy. In 2022, a woman born in Denmark could expect to live 54.4 years free from any activity limitation, compared with 70.3 for a woman in Malta; a range of 15.7 years. In 2022, a man born in Latvia could expect to live 53 years free from any activity limitation, compared with 70.1 for a man in Malta; a gap of 17.1.

The expected number of healthy life years at birth was higher for women than for men in 19 of the EU countries. The difference between genders was generally relatively small: there were 4 EU countries where the gap rose to more than 3.0 years in favor of women (Bulgaria, Lithuania, Slovenia, and Poland) and one where the gap rose to more than 3.0 years in favor of men (the Netherlands). Over the period 2015–2022, the number of healthy years has hardly increased, much less than life expectancy.

[3] EC (2025)

Table 2.5 Life expectancy (LE) and alternative measures of healthy life expectancy (HLE)

Countries			Men			Women		
	LE	HLE GALI	HLE ADL	HLE CASP	LE	HLE GALI	HLE ADL	HLE CASP
Sweden	81.9	77.9	80.7	80	85	79.2	83.3	82.3
Germany	80.1	74.	78.1	77.2	84.4	76.3	81.2	80.8
France	81.3	76	79.5	77.7	86.7	79.9	83.8	81.1
Spain	81.4	79.2	79.2	73.9	86.5	82.9	81.9	76.6
Italy	81.9	77.1	79.9	69.4	86	78.6	82	73.1
Poland	76.5	70.5	74.3	71.1	82.7	74.6	78.9	73.7

Flawinne et al. (2024)

To assess future needs of LTC, it would be interesting to forecast the evolution of disability free life expectancy. A recent study[4] covering 202 countries shows that in industrialized/developed countries such as the USA, Canada, Japan, Germany, France, United Kingdom, and Australia, the increase in HLE is not as substantial, mostly falling in the intermediate or lower range, for both genders.

Flawinne et al. (2024) compare healthy life expectancy using three dependency indicators. In addition to the previously mentioned GALI, they rely on a functional indicator measuring the number of limitations in activities of daily living (ADL) and a more subjective indicator focusing on quality of life (CASP for Control, Autonomy, Self-Realization and Pleasure). These measures come from the European survey SHARE (Survey of Health, Aging and Retirement in Europe). A disability is determined when a person has at least two ADL limitations. Since the prevalence is significantly higher for GALI than for ADL, healthy life expectancy calculated with GALI is systematically lower, regardless of the country or age, than those based on ADL, with the exception of Italian women. The results obtained with CASP vary considerably, and in Italy and Spain, the estimated life expectancy is even lower than with GALI (Table 2.5).

The most striking finding of this study is the weak correlation between the three methods of defining disability. For example, individuals with high scores in Activities of Daily Living (ADL) may score poorly on the CASP or GALI scales. In other words, a person may experience multiple activity limitations and yet feel relatively content, while an autonomous individual might report significant unhappiness. This highlights the complex challenge of defining needs related to states of dependence.

These alternative HLE measures highlight a compelling tension in our approach. Policy makers require standardized metrics like GALI that can effectively guide public policy design and resource allocation. However, if our ultimate goal is maximizing well-being among disabled elderly individuals, the CASP indicator—with its focus on quality of life dimensions—may offer more meaningful insights for achieving that objective.

[4] Cai et al. (2023).

Whereas Healthy Life Expectancy (HLE) measures the average number of years a person can expect to live in good health, free from disability or disease, Disability-Adjusted Life Years (DALYs) represent the total burden of disease by combining years of life lost due to premature death and years lived with disability. These two metrics incorporate the concept of living with disability or poor health, but they measure different aspects of population health. In practical terms, interventions that reduce DALYs in a population (like disease prevention programs) typically increase HLE, and countries with lower DALY rates generally have higher HLE.

2.3 The Triple Penalty: A Cycle of Poverty, Poor Health, and Shortened Life

Whatever the way disability is measured, everywhere, we witness the phenomenon of a "triple penalty," a concept that underscores a profound socioeconomic inequality, where poverty amplifies the challenges of living a shorter life and enduring poorer health for a more significant portion of that life. This phenomenon is a stark reminder of how interconnected economic status, health, and longevity are. The triple penalty is not just additive; it's synergistic. First, poverty increases stress, which worsens health, leading to higher mortality risks. Second, health problems reinforce poverty by reducing income-generating potential, compounding financial hardship. Finally, shorter life expectancy limits opportunities to escape poverty through long-term strategies like education and career advancement.

The triple penalty is a stark indicator of systemic inequality, revealing that societal interventions must target not just health or income alone but the interplay between poverty, health, and longevity. Addressing it holistically is essential for fostering equitable opportunities and improving overall well-being. Whereas there exists a rich literature on the relation between longevity and income/wealth, there is little work devoted to the correlation between disability in old age and socio-economic status. The rich live longer than the poor, and since sources of dependency, such as Alzheimer's disease or chronic illnesses, are linked to old age, one might expect dependency to increase with wealth. However, this is not the case. Recent studies show that the poor experience dependency for longer periods than the rich. The inverse relationship between wealth and dependency (or the fact that wealthier individuals are generally less dependent as they age) can be explained by a combination of socio-economic, environmental, and health-related factors.

First, wealthy individuals have better access to preventive and curative healthcare, such as regular medical check-ups to detect and treat chronic diseases early, or access to specialists and advanced treatments that reduce complications leading to loss of autonomy. In contrast, lower-income populations often face financial barriers to accessing these services, delaying treatment and increasing the risk of dependency. Secondly, affluent individuals generally live in safer and more suitable environments. Their homes are better equipped to prevent accidents (secured staircases, adapted showers, etc.). They also benefit more from green spaces and infrastructures that promote regular physical activity, whereas less wealthy individuals often live in precarious or overcrowded housing, which increases the risk of falls or illnesses. Another reason is that wealthier individuals often lead healthier lifestyles: balanced diets with access to higher-quality food, regular physical activity that maintains their physical condition and delays mobility loss, and fewer risky behaviors such as smoking or excessive alcohol consumption. On the other hand, people in precarious situations are more exposed to lower-quality food (high in sugar and fats) and sedentary lifestyles due to a lack of resources or information. Moreover, individuals with higher education levels have a better understanding of preventive practices. Finally, and likely the most significant factor, wealthy individuals typically hold jobs that are less physically demanding, reducing the likelihood of injuries and musculoskeletal disorders as they age. Meanwhile, workers from modest backgrounds are often exposed to strenuous working conditions, leading to accumulated health problems that increase the probability of dependency (osteoarthritis, chronic fatigue, etc.). .

Among the few existing studies, we have Lefèbvre et al. (2018), who analyze, using data from the Survey of Health, Ageing and Retirement in Europe (SHARE), the relationship between wealth, the subjective survival probability and the probability to become dependent among Europeans aged 50 and above. They find that individuals from the low end of the wealth distribution have a higher probability of becoming dependent and also that they remain dependent longer.

More recently, Connolly et al. (2024) using 2016 Canadian survey data on adults aged between 50 and 70 do find that income and the probability to live to age 85 are positively related while income and the probability to suffer from ADL limitations are negatively related. They also find that while the objective probability to enter a nursing home is negatively correlated with income, the subjective probability is positively correlated with income.

Finally, using HRS and SHARE data, Lefèbvre et al. (2025), study the causal impact of the socio-economic status on disability in old age and its duration. They provide evidence that people with lower economic status are more likely to become disabled and once they are disabled, the duration of their loss of autonomy is higher than that of wealthier individuals.

Those results call for important policy recommendations. Poorer individuals are those who are more likely to become dependent and as such, more generous long-term care (LTC) public policies should primarily be targeted toward them. This would generate a double benefit: first, by reducing the expected cost of dependency for those who would have more difficulty to pay for LTC expenditures and second, by fostering redistribution and decreasing income inequalities across the elderly. Furthermore, we know that occupational health hazards often contribute to reduced life expectancy and lower quality of life for workers in harsh or physically demanding jobs. One could add that low-income earners tend to have high-risk jobs, including jobs in LTC. This should induce public authorities into regulating the labor market to prevent the costly and painful implications of harsh occupations.

References

Belmonte, M., Grubanov-Boskovic, S., Natale, F., Conte, A., Belanger, A., & Sabourin, P. (2023). *Demographic microsimulation of long-term care needs in the European Union*, Publications Office of the European Union. https://doi.org/10.2760/941182, JRC135303

Cai, J., et al. (2023). Healthy life expectancy for 202 countries up to 2030: Projections with a Bayesian model ensemble. *Journal of Global Health, 13*, 04185.

Costa-font, J., Courbage, C., & Swartz, K. (2015). Financing long-term care: Ex ante, ex post or both? *Health Economics, 24*, 45–57.

EC. (2024). *The 2024 ageing report*. Economic and Budgetary Publications Office of the European Union.

EC. (2025). Healthy life years statistics, Eurostat. https://ec.europa.eu/eurostat/statistics-explained/index.php?title=Healthy_life_years_statistics

Flawinne, X., Perelman, S., & Schoenmaeckers, J. (2024). Indicateurs de dépendance sur base de l" enquête share : réflexions sur l" espérance de vie en bonne santé. Revue d" Economie Financière, n0 152.

Lefèbvre, M., Perelman, S., & Schoenmaeckers, J. (2018). Inégalités face la mort et au risque de dépendance. *Revue fran aise d" économie, 33*(2), 75–11.

Lefèbvre, M., Schoenmaeckers, J. & Heymans, L. (2025) Impact of socioeconomic status on loss of autonomy in the old age, unpublished.

Marois, G., & Aktas, A. (2021). Projecting health-ageing trajectories in Europe using a dynamic microsimulation model. *Scientific Reports, 11*(1), 1785.

OECD (2023a). Health at a Glance 2023, OECD, Paris.

OECD (2023b). Pensions at a Glance 2023, OECD, Paris.

Chapter 3
The Market, the State, and the Family

3.1 The Market

The market plays a significant role in providing long-term care for the elderly, encompassing a range of services and facilities designed to meet the health, social, and daily needs of individuals who have a reduced degree of self-sufficiency due to aging. Many long-term care facilities, such as nursing homes, assisted living communities, and home health care services, are operated by private companies. These businesses offer tailored care services that can often provide higher quality amenities and more personalized care compared to some public options, depending on the resources and regulations of a particular country.

Furthermore, the private sector often drives innovation in the field of elderly care. This includes the development of medical technologies, tele-health services, and assistive technologies designed to improve the quality of life for the elderly and increase the efficiency of care services. Innovations such as wearable health monitors, emergency alert systems, and AI-driven health management tools are examples of market contributions that enhance long-term care.

Finally, the market could play a crucial role by offering long-term care insurance products that can help cover the cost of care. These products are particularly significant as they provide financial planning tools that enable individuals to manage the potentially high costs associated with long-term care. The market for these insurance products varies widely across countries, influenced by factors such as demographic trends, cultural attitudes toward familial caregiving, and government policy. Overall, the insurance market does not play an important role in most countries. Here below, we focus on this aspect of the involvement of the market in LTC.

P. Pestieau, *The Economics of Long-term Care*, Developments in Health Economics and Public Policy 14, https://doi.org/10.1007/978-3-032-18237-1_3

3.1.1 *The LTC Insurance Puzzle*

Probably, the most discussed issue when it comes to private LTC insurance is the so-called LTC insurance puzzle,[1] namely the surprising lack of demand for this type of insurance. Indeed, it is widely accepted that the need for LTC is an insurable risk. It concerns the majority of individuals. It can be defined and measured. As a greater number of elderly people will be living longer and face the risk of dependence in the coming years, the benefits of insuring against this risk from a variety of perspectives, including that of the disabled individual and his or her family caregiver, should be compelling. And yet, in the USA, only 3% of LTC expenditures are funded by private LTC insurance. Also, only about 7 million out of 86 million people aged 55 and over have private LTC insurance (Nordman, 2016). Furthermore, the thinness of the LTC insurance market is more prevailing in the other OECD member countries.[2]

How can we explain the lack of demand for an insurance that covers a risk to which the majority of individuals are confronted? The usual reasons for such a weak demand include adverse selection, moral hazard and the offer of public programs that may crowd out private demand for coverage. To these explanations, we could add a number of other factors: unattractive rules of reimbursement, state-dependent preferences as well as behavioral biases and lack of information.

3.1.1.1 High Prices and Adverse Selection

Research by Brown and Finkelstein (2007, 2008, 2009) reveals critical structural challenges in the U.S. long-term care insurance market, centering on gender-based pricing disparities and substantial loading factors that constrain market growth. Their analysis demonstrates a paradoxical pricing dynamic: despite women receiving actuarially favorable rates—sometimes even negative loads that represent below-cost pricing—they do not respond by purchasing more comprehensive coverage. This counterintuitive pattern suggests that factors beyond price, such as information asymmetries or behavioral barriers, fundamentally limit market participation. The loading factor analysis exposes the market's inherent inefficiencies. These "loads"—representing the gap between premiums collected and expected benefit payouts—reach substantial levels when accounting for policy lapses. A 65-year-old male purchaser faces a 44-cent load per premium dollar, effectively paying $1.44 for every dollar of expected benefits. Conversely, women may encounter negative loads, receiving more in expected value than they pay in premiums.

Sloan and Norton (1997) find that asymmetric information as to the probability of turning disabled leads to adverse selection and explains part of these high prices. The demand for LTC insurance depends on various observable factors associated with age, health, and functional status as well as unobservable ones such as individuals' subjective probability of future nursing home use. This probability rests in part on

[1] Pestieau and Ponthiere (2012).

[2] See, for example, OECD (2020).

the degree of aversion to being in a nursing home of the individuals and on their impressions about the availability of their families and friends to help them if they become severely dependent. This probability is private information. To the extent that the person's own knowledge about future use differs from the insurer's observation, there is the potential for adverse selection.

A number of authors (Brown and Warshawsky, 2013; De Donder et al., 2022; Murtaugh et al., 2001) argue in favor of integrating LTC insurance with life annuities. Such a combination of insurance against two negatively correlated risks (longevity and disability) would reduce the costs and the extent of adverse selection for both products since those in bad health are likely to face higher prices for LTC insurance but lower prices for annuities (due to their higher mortality) and vice versa. De Donder et al. (2022) show that this kind of bundling could even result in advantageous selection.[3]

3.1.1.2 Moral Hazard

Pauly (1990) develops a particular type of moral hazard for private LTC insurance, the so-called intra-family moral hazard. Accordingly, elderly persons fear that if they purchase private insurance, children may tend to send them in nursing homes as soon as they are unable to act on their own. Insurance may indeed induce such a move as it reduces the cost of institutionalization relative to the cost of giving personal attention. Elderly persons who prefer informal care from their children over formal care may therefore choose not to purchase insurance. Zweifel and StrÃ¼we (1998) demonstrate that when parents purchase long-term care (LTC) insurance, it often reduces the amount of care provided by their primary caregivers, typically children who earn relatively low wages. Due to this moral hazard effect, parents are often predicted to forgo purchasing LTC insurance. See also Zweifel and Courbage (2016) and Klimaviciute (2017, 2019).

On the question of moral hazard, Trainar (2024) challenges the prevailing notion that dependence risk is readily insurable. He highlights the inherent ambiguity associated with this type of risk. Consequently, contracts designed to mitigate dependence risk often display a fundamental asymmetry, thereby creating potential for moral hazard.

3.1.1.3 Availability of Social Assistance

The availability of social assistance such as Medicaid in the USA may crowd out demand for private LTC insurance. Medicaid is designed to provide coverage only for the very poor. To qualify, one must have virtually no non-housing wealth. However, there is considerable evidence that to qualify for Medicaid, middle-class elderly

[3] They define advantageous selection as the situation when a rise in the insurance premium induces high-cost individuals to leave the market, which decreases the average cost among those who remain.

persons become impoverished by spending all their wealth during a nursing home stay, a process called spend-down. According to Wiener et al. (2013) who analyze a population of elderly over the period 1996–2008, almost 10% of the previously non-Medicaid population aged 50 and over spent down to Medicaid eligibility.[4] There is further such a thing as "artificial self-impoverishment," which involves manipulating one's income and assets so that an individual who would otherwise not qualify for Medicaid LTC benefits can slip in below the financial eligibility limits and qualify after all. One standard technique of such strategic impoverishment consists in transferring one's assets to relatives at less than fair market value for the purpose of appearing artificially poor.[5] This being said, Kim (2018) has shown that eliminating the Medicaid program increases LTC insurance holding by only 5.3%,[6] which implies that the demand for LTC insurance would remain low even without Medicaid. In the next chapter, we come back on this issue.[7]

3.1.1.4 State-Dependent Preferences

A further explanation for the underdeveloped disability insurance market centers on preference shifts that occur following disability. The argument suggests that individuals who become disabled experience a decline in the marginal utility of income, which paradoxically reduces their demand for the very insurance that would have protected them. This view is theoretically justified by assuming that disability makes an individual less efficient in transforming income into utility.

De Donder and Leroux (2021) indicate that if old age disability decreases the marginal utility of daily life consumption, then there is less need for insurance. As they show, on the one hand, dependency creates additional expenses (LTC costs), which calls for buying insurance, but, on the other hand, if daily life consumption becomes less valuable when dependent, there is less incentive to transfer resources to the bad state of nature, namely in case of disability. The individual's decision of whether to buy insurance depends on the relative size of the two effects, but even if insurance is purchased, it is then optimal to insure less than fully.

To date, the empirical literature on state-dependent preferences in the context of loss of autonomy has failed to reach a consensus. In part, this is due to specification differences. On the one hand, Lillard and Weiss (1997) and Ameriks et al. (2020) find that marginal utility is higher when dependent than when autonomous. On the other hand, Finkelstein et al. (2013) and Koijen et al. (2016) obtain that the marginal utility of consumption decreases in the case of poor health, which would explain the LTC insurance puzzle.

Let us remember a basic principle of insurance: for a risk to be worth insuring, the marginal utility of wealth should be higher in the loss state than in the no-loss

[4] We come back on this issue in the following chapter.

[5] See Wiener et al. (2017).

[6] The share of individuals in the sample having LTC insurance increases from 9.5 to 10%.

[7] See Norton (1995).

state, which creates a demand for insurance. In other words, people would buy a LTC insurance when the marginal utility of money is higher in bad states (in case of disability) than in good states (when fully autonomous).

3.1.1.5 Behavioral Biases and Lack of Information

Concepts from behavioral economics such as "loss aversion" (the idea that losses loom larger than gains) might make people reluctant to spend money on an insurance product that they hope never to use. Furthermore, the "optimism bias" (the belief that bad things are less likely to happen to oneself than to others) might lead people to underestimate their own need for future care. Also, psychological factors such as procrastination and present bias (a preference for immediate rewards over future benefits) also play a role. Purchasing long-term care insurance is easy to put off because the benefits are not immediate and are contingent upon an unpleasant future possibility—becoming severely dependent. Another reason why individuals tend to under-save for retirement and particularly for LTC may be lack of information and knowledge. Empirical studies such as Zhou-Richter et al. (2010) or Boyer et al. (2019, 2019) document these effects. Finally, it can arise from present bias and self-control problems. Accordingly, individuals would have two selves, one concerned by instant gratification and another by long-term benefits and later well-being. When choosing how much to save, the first self would prevail. Clearly, those behavioral biases could be invoked to explain the low demand for LTC insurance. Cremer and Roeder (2013) and De Donder and Leroux (2013) show that these biases can affect the design of optimal LTC policies.

3.1.1.6 Denial of Severe Dependence

Many individuals underestimate the likelihood that they will need long-term care. This form of cognitive bias—where people believe that they are less likely to experience negative events compared to others—is widespread. The reality, however, is quite different. Studies suggest that about 70% of people turning age 65 can expect to use some form of long-term care during their lives. Denial or minimization of this fact can lead people to forego preparing for such eventualities. Kopchuk and Slemrod (2005) show that attempts to reduce death anxiety and the possibility of denial of mortality-relevant information interact with intertemporal choices and may lead to time-inconsistent behavior and other behavioral phenomena. Individuals seem to have the same denial attitude toward such an unpleasant occurrence as dementia or heavy and lasting disability in old age.

3.1.2 Unappealing Rules of Reimbursement

Long-term care insurance policies can be complex, and many people find it difficult to choose a suitable plan. The current formulas of benefit payments are unattractive. Two countries in which the LTC insurance market has been rather developed so far are the USA and France. In the USA, the formula of reimbursement tended to be the prevailing one up to recently. This formula is based on that used in health care insurance. However, now most companies offer policies of the cash indemnity type within a limited period. In France, the common formula is that of the lifetime cash indemnity. The rule of reimbursement of LTC insurance most used currently in the USA that provides benefits for a given period is unappealing as it does not cover cases where the disabled elderly lives beyond that period. Conditions like Alzheimer's disease, stroke, or other chronic illnesses can require care for many years, sometimes a decade or more. A person might exhaust their policy benefits while still needing extensive care. The lump-sum approach used in France tends to offer an insufficient coverage in case of heavy disability.

The relative desirability of those payment rules depends on the underlying assumptions. For instance, when family assistance is introduced, the flat lump-sum payment seems to be more efficient. See on this Cremer, Lozachmeur and Pestieau) (2016) and Klimaviciute (2017). It remains that neither of the two formulas provides sufficient protection against the cost of a severe and long disability, which is not totally unlikely. Nordman (2016) indicates that 52% of individuals turning 65 will have high LTC needs over their remaining lifetimes. These needs are expected to last about 2 years on average, but they will last longer for 26% of individuals. This is especially relevant for women: 17.8% of them will have a period of 5 and more years of severe dependence as it appears on Table 3.1. Also, there seems to be a negative correlation between income and the length of LTC need. For instance, 22% of individuals in the highest income quintile will need LTC for more than 2 years, while the proportion goes up to 31% for those belonging to the lowest income quintile. In an earlier study, Brown and Finkelstein (2008) estimate that about one-third of 65-year olds will enter a nursing home. The length of the nursing home stay is mostly less than 12 months. They show however that 12women will spend more than 3 years at a nursing home. The financial cost for these stays is quite high. According to Genworth CareScout (2024), the 2024 national median monthly cost is $5,900 for assisted living community, $9,277 for a nursing home semi-private room, and $10,646 for a Nursing home private room. These LTC costs increase faster than inflation.

Table 3.1 Length of heavy dependence (USA, age 65+)

	% with LTC needs	None (% of cohort)	<2years	2–5 years	>5years
Men	46.7	55.3	25.8	11.1	9.8
Women	57.5	42.5	27.5	12.3	17.8

Nordman (2016)

To avoid the possibility for a fraction of dependents to spend down all their resources and to be forced to rely on their children's aid or on social assistance such as Medicaid, Drèze et al. (2016) and Klimaviciute and Pestieau (2018a, b) argue in favor of the deductible principle. Accordingly, the individuals would have to pay part of the costs of dependence incurred during a certain number of months, and beyond a certain threshold, all the costs would be covered. Inspired by the famous theorem of the deductible by Arrow (1963), these authors show that such insurance policy is efficient in the case of LTC.[8] Klimaviciute and Pestieau (2020) confirm that the deductible formula for LTC remains relevant under ex post moral hazard as well. Furthermore, Klimaviciute et al. (2020) find that the efficiency of the deductible also holds in the presence of family solidarity, although some departures from the standard results exist in those cases. We come back on these issues in a more formal way in the next chapter.

All in all, the consequences of the ensuing thin LTC insurance market are twofold: it puts further pressure on the family and on the government and it explains why saving is still increasing in old age, which leads to unexpected bequests in case parents escape disability. See on this Ameriks et al. (2020). It appears clear that encouraging more people to purchase long-term care insurance is desirable but requires both education about the risks and potential costs of long-term care, as well as making insurance products more accessible and understandable. Financial education campaigns, simpler product offerings, and possibly government incentives or mandates could help increase the uptake of long-term care insurance.

3.1.3 *Home Ownership as a Surrogate for LTC Insurance*

Acquiring a house is often regarded as one of the most effective strategies for ensuring security and protection in the event of disability in old age.[9] This perspective arises from the multifaceted benefits of homeownership, which extend beyond the immediate utility of having a place to live. A house provides not only a physical shelter but also a sense of stability and independence that is especially critical in later years when physical or financial vulnerabilities may increase. One of the primary reasons a house is considered a safeguard against disability-related challenges is its capacity to eliminate or significantly reduce housing costs in retirement. For individuals who own their homes outright, the absence of rent or mortgage payments means that a significant portion of their monthly expenses is alleviated. This financial stability can make it easier to allocate resources toward healthcare, caregiving, and other essential needs that may arise due to disability.

Furthermore, owning a house enables customization to suit the specific needs of aging individuals. As physical abilities decline, homeowners can modify their living spaces to enhance accessibility and comfort. Features such as wheelchair ramps,

---

[8] See Dilnot (2011).

[9] Achou (2021).

widened doorways, stairlifts, and grab bars can be installed without the constraints or permissions often required in rental properties. This adaptability ensures that the home remains a safe and functional environment, reducing the likelihood of accidents and supporting an individual's desire to age in place. It's important to recognize, though, that some of these investments carry significant expenses that remain uncovered by existing insurance schemes, whether public or private.

In addition to its practical advantages, a house often serves as a valuable financial asset. In cases where medical expenses or long-term care costs become overwhelming, homeowners can tap into the equity built up in their property through options like reverse mortgages, home equity loans, or even selling the house if necessary. This financial cushion provides a critical safety net, helping to manage the unpredictability of old age and disability-related expenses. Homeownership also fosters a sense of community and belonging, which can be particularly beneficial for individuals with disabilities. Living in a familiar neighborhood often means having access to a support network of friends, family, and neighbors who can provide assistance or companionship when needed. This social dimension of owning a home contributes significantly to emotional well-being, which is equally important for maintaining a good quality of life in old age. In contrast, relying on rental housing in old age may introduce uncertainties, such as the potential for rising rents, eviction risks, or the inability to make necessary modifications to the property.

These factors can compound the challenges faced by individuals with disabilities, making homeownership a more appealing and secure option. Thus, acquiring a house stands out as a prudent and effective means of ensuring protection against the uncertainties of disability in old age. It combines financial security, adaptability, and social stability, providing a comprehensive solution that supports both physical and emotional well-being. This long-term investment not only safeguards against immediate challenges but also empowers individuals to face the future with confidence and dignity. Selling your home can provide a significant financial resource to fund your stay in a nursing home for several years. The proceeds from the sale of your home often convert a significant portion of your net worth into liquid assets, which can then be used to cover the monthly costs of long-term care. Given that nursing home expenses typically range in the USA between $7,000 and $10,000 per month,[10] depending on the location and level of care, the equity you've built in your home may be sufficient to support these expenses for an extended period. For those who are not ready to sell immediately, alternative options like renting out the property to generate a steady income stream or using a reverse mortgage to tap into the equity while retaining ownership may provide interim solutions. Emotional and practical considerations, such as attachment to the home or the need to store or distribute belongings, should also be factored into the decision-making process.

Finally, if there is a possibility that a nursing home stay could be temporary, selling the home might not be the most flexible solution, and short-term financing options might be worth exploring. A substantial body of literature, primarily from the

[10] In European countries such as France and Germany, the costs are quite lower: between 4000 and 5000 euros.

USA, highlights the role of illiquid housing assets in financing long-term care and potentially substituting for long-term care insurance. Research indicates that retirees primarily deplete housing wealth when transitioning to LTC facilities. According to Davidoff (2010), older adults often hold significant wealth in home equity, which is rarely utilized before death unless they move into LTC facilities. The illiquid nature of home equity may discourage the purchase of private LTC insurance by serving dual functions. First, it provides a buffer of assets that can be liquidated to cover care costs if needed. Second, it increases the marginal utility of liquid wealth, which might otherwise be allocated to insurance premiums. Venti and Wise (2004) observe that, aside from public pensions, housing equity represents the principal asset for a large proportion of older Americans, many of whom have minimal financial assets to sustain retirement consumption. Homeownership can be a critical financial resource for meeting LTC needs, particularly through mechanisms like home-equity conversion or reverse mortgages. These options allow individuals to access the equity in their homes to cover LTC expenses, effectively serving as a substitute for traditional LTC insurance.

Chen (2001) extensively examines the use of home equity to support LTC, emphasizing the potential of reverse mortgages to enhance financial security for older adults confronting care needs. Similarly, Hanewald et al. (2020) explore various strategies for unlocking housing wealth to fund LTC. Their analysis underscores the straightforward approach of selling property and using the proceeds to cover LTC insurance premiums or direct care costs. However, they also highlight the challenges associated with this method, such as relocation requirements and the potential impact on family members. In conclusion, leveraging home equity through mechanisms like reverse mortgages offers a viable alternative or supplement to LTC insurance. This approach provides a flexible financial solution for addressing care needs in later life, thereby mitigating some of the limitations associated with traditional insurance options.

3.2 The Family

Since the dawn of time, the family has been the main provider of LTC in our societies. Much more than the state and surely more than the market. Yet, in spite of increasing needs, its role seems to be decreasing due to several interrelated factors, primarily driven by demographic, social, and economic changes. Following increased in life expectancy and declining fertility, most countries are experiencing aging populations. This shift increases the demand for care, but the simultaneous decrease in birth rates means there are fewer family members available to provide that care. Traditional family structures have evolved. There are more single-parent families, smaller families, and families where both adults work full-time, which can limit the ability of family members to provide extensive care. Additionally, the increase in divorce rates and remarriages can complicate familial obligations and responsibilities. There is a cultural shift in some societies toward individualism and self-reliance, which can decrease the perceived responsibility to care for elders within one's own family. Moreover, societal attitudes toward professional eldercare facilities have become more favorable, making them a more acceptable option. These factors contribute to a decreasing reliance on family for eldercare, reshaping how societies care for their aging populations. This trend necessitates a revaluation of policies and practices surrounding eldercare to address the needs of both the elderly and their families effectively.

3.2.1 Contribution of the Family to LTC

Despite demographic shifts and changing family structures, informal caregiving remains the backbone of long-term care (LTC) for elderly individuals, with family members providing an estimated 80% of all care hours. Spouses, partners, and adult children constitute the primary caregiving network, with women—particularly wives and daughters—shouldering a disproportionate share of these responsibilities. While this pattern is well-documented across cultures, collecting precise data on informal caregiving presents significant methodological challenges due to the private nature of care provision and variations in how caregiving activities are defined and reported. The measurement of family caregiving contributions requires a multidimensional framework that captures both tangible and intangible aspects of care. Key dimensions include time allocation (direct care hours and supervision), financial expenditures (out-of-pocket costs and lost wages), emotional labor (psychological support and stress management), and care quality indicators (safety, consistency, and appropriateness of care). Researchers employ mixed-method approaches to assess these components, combining quantitative tools such as time-use surveys and economic analyses with qualitative methods including in-depth interviews and observational studies. This comprehensive assessment typically incorporates perspectives from multiple stakeholders: family caregivers, care recipients, healthcare professionals, and social workers, providing a more complete picture of the caregiving landscape.

To assess the size of informal care provided by the family, one uses the same method that is employed to measure the contribution of household work to GDP. Admittedly, this is a complex task because traditional GDP only includes market transactions—activities that have a market price. Household work, such as cooking, cleaning, childcare, and eldercare, though economically significant, is generally unpaid and therefore not included in standard GDP calculations. However, there are methods and approaches economists use to estimate its value. They generally consist of two stages. First, they rely upon Time Use Surveys (TUS) that collect data on how individuals allocate their time to various activities, including unpaid household work. These surveys provide insights into the amount of time spent on household tasks. Second, these methods estimate the value of household work by calculating how much it would cost to hire someone to perform the same tasks. It involves estimating the market wage rate for professionals providing similar services (e.g., housekeepers, chefs, nannies) and then multiplying the time spent on each task by the corresponding wage rate.

For example, a study by McKinsey[11] estimated that unpaid work contributes around $10 trillion annually to the global economy, representing nearly 13% of global GDP if it were included. Several studies have quantified the economic significance of informal care in the USA. Coe et al. (2018) estimated its value at $277 billion in 2011 alone. Building on this research, Coe and Werner (2022) examined informal caregiving within residential care facilities and nursing homes, demonstrating that its contribution remains substantial even in institutional settings. Van Houtven et al. (2013) provide additional evidence supporting the considerable economic impact of informal care arrangements.

In a recent study (EC, 2021), an evaluation of the significance of informal care in the EU is presented, measured as a percentage of GDP. The authors employ two approaches to estimate this value: the proxy-good method, which assigns a monetary value to informal caregivers' time based on the market price of professional substitutes for specific caregiving tasks, and the opportunity cost method, which values the time of informal caregivers based on the potential earnings or alternative uses of that time foregone.

Table 3.2 compares the value of informal long-term care provision in percentage of GDP. It is calculated using these two methods. Additionally, it includes the value of formal LTC expenditures as reported in the Ageing Report. Two key observations emerge from these figures. First, in most Member States, the value of informal care surpasses public LTC expenditures. Second, Southern European countries, including France, appear to benefit from substantial levels of informal care, despite (or because) relatively low levels of public spending on formal LTC.

This market-replacement approach fundamentally diverges from the well-being valuation method (Costa-Font & Vilaplana-Prieto, 2024; Schneider & Kleindienst, 2016), which incorporates a comprehensive assessment of caregivers' welfare impacts, including both positive aspects (emotional satisfaction, strengthened family bonds) and negative outcomes (stress, career disruptions). The methodology used in EC (2021) adopts a more focused scope, specifically calculating the market equivalent value of informal care hours provided by family members to elderly and disabled relatives. The resulting valuations are consistently higher than those derived from the well-being approach, primarily because the market-replacement method does not account for the economic costs of caregiving.

[11] https://apolitical.co/solution-articles/en/how-to-value-unpaid-care-work-the-10-trillion-question.

Table 3.2 Informal care and public LTC spending as % of GDP.

I			
	Proxy good	Opportunity cost	Public spending
France	5	4.2	1.9
Spain	4.9	3.7	0.7
Greece	3.9	2.7	0.2
Italy	3.6	2.9	1.7
Netherlands	1.5	1.4	3.7
Sweden	1.6	1.6	3.3
Germany	0.9	0.8	1.6
EU27	2.7	2.4	1.7

EC (2021)

3.2.2 Care Motives

Children often care for their disabled parents for a variety of reasons rooted in emotional, social, cultural, and practical factors. The three main reasons that can be combined are altruism, family norm, and reciprocity or exchange.

One of the primary reasons children care for their disabled parents is altruism, namely, the deep emotional bond and love they share. The instinct to care for one's parents can be seen as a natural response to the nurturing they received as children. Altruistic children find a deep sense of personal satisfaction and fulfillment in caring for their parents. They are not compelled and do not seek any reward.

Another reason is reciprocity and exchange. Many children feel a sense of reciprocity—they want to give back to their parents who spent years providing for and nurturing them. Caring for a disabled parent can be seen as a way to express gratitude and to return the care that was once given to them. With three or even four generation families, one observes a sort of implicit compact. Grandparents help their grand-children and when they turn disabled, they are cared for by their own children. There are different types of compacts, on which we come back below.

In many societies, there are specific cultural norms and expectations regarding the care of the elderly or disabled family members. It is expected that children will take on the primary caregiving role, rather than utilizing institutional care. This norm can be constricting and thus have some negative implications on the health of the caregivers.

Let us add that in some countries, there are laws that obligate adult children to care for their aging parents, which can also play a role in why children take on these responsibilities. In any case, each family's situation is unique, and the decision to care for a disabled parent involves a complex interplay of these and other factors. For example, in France, there is a clear legal obligation for adult children to financially support their aging parents through what's called "l'obligation alimentaire" (maintenance obligation). This obligation extends beyond just parents to include grandparents and other direct ascendants. It covers essential needs like food, housing, clothing, and medical care when parents cannot afford these necessities themselves. Parents can request a maintenance allowance from their children, particularly for care-related expenses. These filial responsibility laws are actively enforced, making it a genuine legal duty rather than just a family expectation.

Klimaviciute et al. (2017) test alternative models of long-term caring motives. They consider three canonical motives: pure altruism, exchange and family norm. Their database is the second wave of the Survey of Health, Ageing and Retirement in Europe (SHARE), which allows linking almost perfectly and with complete information children and their parents' characteristics. Comparing the empirical results to the theoretical models developed, it appears that, depending on the regions analyzed, long-term caring is driven by moderate altruism or by family norm. In contrast, Alessie et al. (2014), also using SHARE data, stress the importance of exchange motive in intergenerational transfers.

3.2.3 Collateral Risks for the Caregivers

Caring for elderly loved ones is a profoundly noble and often rewarding experience, but it can also carry substantial health risks for caregivers. When an individual takes on the role of a caregiver, particularly for an elderly family member, they frequently face a range of challenges that can impact their physical, emotional, and mental health. Understanding these impacts is crucial for caregivers to seek appropriate support and maintain their well-being.

Caregiving often involves physical tasks such as lifting, bathing, and assisting with mobility. These activities can lead to physical strain, injuries, and chronic pain. Caregivers may also experience neglect of their own health needs, leading to further physical health problems. Chronic stress is a common outcome for many caregivers, as they juggle caregiving with other personal and professional commitments. Over time, chronic stress can lead to serious health issues, including hypertension, cardiovascular disease, and weakened immune response. They often experience high levels of emotional and mental health challenges, including depression, anxiety, and feelings of isolation. The emotional burden of caring for someone who may be experiencing significant declines in physical and cognitive health can be profound.

Furthermore, caregivers often isolate themselves or feel cut off from social interactions due to the demands of caregiving. Social isolation can impact mental health, leading to increased risks of mortality and conditions like heart disease and dementia. The cumulative effect of long-term caregiving can lead to burnout—a state of physical, emotional, and mental exhaustion. Burnout can cause caregivers to feel less capable of providing care and may affect their overall sense of self and purpose.

To mitigate these impacts, caregivers must acknowledge the challenges and seek support where possible. This can include tapping into resources such as local support groups, respite care services, counseling, and seeking help from other family members or professional services. It's also crucial for caregivers to maintain their health through regular check-ups, healthy lifestyle choices, and setting aside time for personal rest and recreation. Recognizing the signs of stress and seeking help early is essential for both the well-being of the caregiver and the quality of care they can provide to their loved one. It can lead him or more often her to consider alternatives such as institutionalizing the dependent parent or spouse.

Those collateral effects of caregiving have received much attention in recent work. First, as shown by Schulz and Sherwood (2008) as well as Van Houtven et al. (2013), family caregiving has a number of negative impacts on the health and the career of helpers. The negative effects seem to increase with the severity of the dependence particularly in case of dementia. They are expected to be more important when the motive is the family norm and not altruism. Stöckel and Bom (2022) estimate the longer-term and dynamic effects of providing informal care on caregivers' health in the UK. Their results suggest substantial negative health effects confined to the mental domain and asymmetrically experienced by caregivers providing more than 20 h of weekly care. Furthermore, for caregivers providing multiple years of higher intensity care, the negative effects persist.

Health issues can result in a lack of stability in care provision, which may serve as a compelling argument in favor of institutionalization. Drawing on data from the 2010–2018 waves of the Health and Retirement Study, Angrisani et al. (2025) examine how the stability of informal care influences depressive symptoms among older adults with ongoing care needs and how it mitigates the stress associated with limitations in activities of daily living (ADL) and instrumental activities of daily living (IADL). Their findings indicate that stable informal care is strongly linked to lower levels of depressive symptoms. Moreover, stability in care significantly reduces stress stemming from IADL limitations, offering protective benefits for mental health. This underscores the critical importance of long-term commitment to caregiving for the well-being of individuals with chronic care needs.

The institutional and policy contexts play a role in determining caregiving experiences. Kaschowitz and Brandt (2017) emphasize that caregiving outcomes vary not only across welfare regimes but even among countries with similar welfare state models. Additional evidence suggests that women in Southern European welfare states tend to experience higher levels of caregiving-related stress compared to those in Northern welfare regimes, where more robust public care systems can mitigate the burden (Brenna & Di Novi, 2016). However, much of the existing research in this area relies on cross-sectional data, which limits the ability to capture the dynamic nature of caregiving or to account for selection effects. As Vlachantoni et al. (2013) argue, longitudinal data methods are essential to estimate the causal impact of caregiving on health and well-being in a more accurate way. Recently, using SHARE data, Chaves Araujo et al. (2025) observe limited average health impacts, with only a short-run decline in quality of life for low-intensity carers.

3.2.4 Strategic Interaction Among Family Members

The long-term care literature offers several theoretical and empirical studies dealing with the strategic interaction among family members. These studies vary along several dimensions: which family members participate in the decision-making process, which types of care and/or living arrangements are considered, whether family members have common preferences, and whether other decisions are determined jointly with long-term care decisions. Given the variety of long-term care arrangements and the connection between care and living arrangements, one model cannot capture all possible aspects of a family's long-term care and living arrangements.

Most of the existing theoretical models involve families consisting of an elderly parent and only one child in the decision-making process. Kotlikoff and Morris (1990) present a model where parent and child decide whether to form an intergenerational household or to maintain separate households. The parent and child solve separate maximization problems if they live separately but maximize a weighted average of their individual utility functions subject to their pooled budget constraint if they live together. In this latter case, the weights are determined by a bargaining process.

With the lengthening of life, more and more families comprise three and even four generations and furthermore, many individuals experience two stages in their old age, one of good health and a lot of leisure and one of disability and dependence. We thus see grandparents who first care for their grandchildren and then go through a stage of disability and dependence and get cared for by their own children. This family compact involving child-care in exchange for eldercare has been analyzed by Lefebvre et al. (2025) using a model with subgame perfect equilibrium with the child acting as a Stackelberg leader. This model is then successfully tested using SHARE data.

In other types of models, more than one adult child in a family participate in the family's long-term care decision. The potential disagreement among adult siblings and between adult children and elderly parents motivates the development of a game-theoretic framework where the players include the parent and all of her children. The players of the game are an elderly parent who is functionally impaired but living independently and her children. The original model in that respect is the strategic bequest one of Bernheim et al. (1985), who consider a setting in which the parent influences the caring decisions of his children by holding wealth in bequeathable forms and by conditioning the division of bequests on the level of care the children are providing. Their model generates robust empirical predictions. The strategic bequest motive has been tested by a number of economists with the conclusion that bequests are often used as compensation for services rendered.

For example, Hiedemann and Stern (1999) model the family's long-term care decision as a two-stage non-cooperative game. The players of the game are an elderly parent who is functionally impaired but living independently and her children. In the first stage of the game, each child simultaneously announces whether she offers to care for the parent. In the second stage, the parent chooses among the available care arrangements. They use data from the National Long-term Care Survey. Their model leads to reasonable estimates of the marginal effects of various parent and child characteristics on caregiving behavior. In particular, it predicts that mothers are more likely than fathers to be cared for by children, married parents are more likely than single parents to live independently, daughters are more likely than sons to care for parents, and family members' valuation of care provided by a child depends negatively on the distance between the parent and the child.

Using a collective choice model of the family and data from SHARE, Canta et al. (2024) deal with the question of the relative contribution of spouses to the long-term care needs of their dependent parents and parents-in-law. Their paper focuses on the role of gender and blood relationships as well as the effect of differential opportunity costs within the couple. The results tend to confirm the existence of gender and blood biases in the level of informal care provided by each spouse, while their wage does not seem to play a large role. When they consider the relative level of informal care by spouses, the gender and blood biases are confirmed. Furthermore, the wage ratio is negatively related to the informal care ratio. These results imply that informal care and private insurance coverage may depend on the gender composition of children, which may justify differentiated public LTC transfers.

The dynamics of eldercare are intrinsically linked to societal structures, with gender roles manifesting distinctly across cultural contexts. While contemporary societies increasingly demonstrate egalitarian care patterns, patriarchal environments reveal more nuanced familial support mechanisms. In a compelling recent investigation, Ho and McGarry (2025) illuminate the intricate landscape of intergenerational transfers within China's traditional familial framework. Their research unveils a gendered pattern of parental support that is both striking and systematic. Sons emerge as the primary providers of substantial, coresidential assistance, monopolizing both significant financial transfers and residential care. Daughters, by contrast, tend to contribute through more modest, typically smaller-scale transfers. Perhaps most intriguing is the researchers' observation of intra-gender transfer dynamics. When siblings of the same gender increase in number, a pronounced "crowding-out" effect emerges: sons reduce their contributions when brothers proliferate, while daughters similarly diminish support in the presence of additional sisters. Notably, this pattern remains consistent across both in-kind and monetary transfers, suggesting a deep-rooted gender-specific approach to familial support that transcends even relatively fungible forms of assistance.

3.2.5 Strategic Impoverishment

Most countries have LTC programs for the low-income elderly. The best known of these programs is the U.S. Medicaid that provides an important safety net for people who are poor or become poor, either because of the high costs of health and long-term care services or for other reasons. Indeed, some individuals reduce their countable assets in order to qualify for Medicaid. This is referred to as spending down assets for Medicaid. Many other countries have needs-based program such as Medicaid, meaning applicants must meet strict income and asset limits to qualify. For budgetary reasons, they also face the need of discouraging individuals from spending down their assets to qualify for their benefits.

This behavior has been labeled "strategic impoverishment." Medicaid has both income and asset limits, which vary by state, but in most cases, individuals can only have a few thousand dollars in "countable" assets to qualify. Assets such as cash, savings, investments, and certain property are considered countable, while some assets, like a primary home (up to a value limit), a car, and personal belongings, may be exempt. There are unavoidable reasons for spending down: paying for medical expenses, long-term care, or other healthcare costs. There are also reasons that could be avoided such as purchasing exempt assets, like home modifications or a car, or transferring assets to family members. There exist some ways to discourage or mitigate asset spend-down for Medicaid. First of all, encouraging individuals to purchase private long-term care insurance can help them cover the costs of care without needing to rely on Medicaid. In the same vein, promoting financial planning that incorporates healthcare costs in retirement, such as opening Health Savings Accounts or other tax-advantaged savings vehicles could encourage people to save more for healthcare in retirement rather than relying on Medicaid.

Another way is to penalize individuals who transfer assets within a certain "look-back period" (typically five years). Tightening these rules or extending the look-back period could further discourage individuals from gifting or transferring assets to family members in order to qualify for Medicaid. Some argue that Medicaid eligibility thresholds for long-term care are too low, forcing people to spend down their assets. Raising asset and income thresholds would reduce the need for individuals to impoverish themselves to qualify for benefits. At the same time, such a policy would increase the budgetary pressures on the program. Finally, there is the idea of offering Medicaid Partnership Programs that allow individuals to keep more of their assets while still qualifying for Medicaid if they have long-term care insurance. Expanding these programs could reduce the incentive to spend down assets while still providing care. Each of these approaches involves balancing the protection of individuals' financial security with the need to ensure fair access to healthcare. For any reforms, it's essential to consider potential unintended consequences, such as increasing the financial burden on middle-class families or reducing access to care for low-income individuals without neglecting the budgetary cost of the programs. In the remaining of this paper, we focus on the budgetary issue showing that both increasing the look back period or decreasing the asset threshold can contribute to decreasing the number of users of Medicaid and thus to relax the financial constraints to which today governments are subject in rapidly aging societies.

There is a growing empirical literature that examines the hypothesis that individuals may strategically offload assets to meet the eligibility requirements of means-tested long-term care (LTC) public programs. Much of this research focuses on the U.S. Medicaid system and investigates the effects of eligibility restrictions on factors such as the number of Medicaid applicants, personal savings, and intergenerational transfers.

Bassett (2007) finds that individuals' self-assessed probability of entering a nursing home is a significant predictor of their likelihood to transfer assets. Liu and Mukherjee (2020) explore how restricting Medicaid eligibility affects asset transfers to children, showing that these effects are particularly notable for individuals with a high risk of requiring nursing home care. In the same line, Ayyagari and He (2019) find that, in response to more stringent penalties on asset transfers, married seniors with high expectations of future nursing home use significantly modified the structure of their wealth by reducing the countable assets, relative to married seniors with low expectations.

More recently, Lozachmeur et al. (2025) have shown that the Medicaid reform consisting in lengthening the look-back period had the double effect of modifying the temporal profile of inter vivos gifts and decreasing the number of applicants to this program. We come back on this in the next chapter. However, there is no consensus on whether elderly individuals frequently transfer assets to their children to qualify for Medicaid. For instance, Norton (1995) concludes that spending down assets is not a widespread practice, suggesting that the phenomenon may be less prevalent than often assumed.

Finally, note that most countries do have asset-related restrictions for long-term care, but they typically handle it quite differently than the U.S. system. For example, in the United Kingdom there exist capital limits for long-term care assistance. No assistance with costs would be provided where an individual has capital of more than 23,250 and reduced assistance will be provided where capital is between the upper and lower capital limits. However, this system is generally less punitive than the U.S. approach.

3.2.6 Better at Home Than in a Nursing Home?

The decision between moving to a nursing home or staying at home with adequate care for a disabled elderly person involves a complex balance of medical, emotional, and practical considerations. Nursing homes ideally provide a structured environment where professional medical care is available around the clock. This ensures that any chronic health issues or emergencies are managed promptly, and access to specialized services such as physical therapy, rehabilitation, and mental health support is readily available. Additionally, nursing homes offer a social atmosphere that can be beneficial for those who might otherwise experience isolation, with organized activities and opportunities to engage with peers. For family members, placing a loved one in a nursing home can relieve the emotional and physical demands of caregiving, allowing them to focus on maintaining a supportive and loving relationship. On the other hand, staying at home with proper care has distinct advantages, particularly the comfort and emotional stability of being in a familiar environment. This setting allows the elderly individual to maintain a sense of autonomy and independence, with daily routines and personal preferences preserved. Personalized care at home ensures that the specific needs of the individual are met with flexibility, often fostering a stronger bond between the caregiver and the person receiving care. Staying at home can also reduce the stress and potential emotional distress associated with institutional living, which may include adjusting to new surroundings and adhering to structured schedules. Additionally, it allows for closer family involvement, facilitating more natural and frequent interactions with loved ones.

From a financial perspective, while nursing homes can be expensive, the cost of staying at home can vary based on the level of care required, modifications to the home, and the hiring of professional caregivers. Home care can sometimes be more cost-effective, particularly if family members can supplement care or if community resources are available. However, for individuals with complex medical conditions, the comprehensive services provided in a nursing home might outweigh the potential cost savings of home care. Ultimately, the choice between a nursing home and home care depends on the elderly person's medical needs, personal preferences, and the resources available to them and their family. Each option offers unique advantages, and the decision should focus on ensuring the individual's quality of life, comfort, and well-being.

In many countries, recent public policies have increasingly emphasized home- and community-based care for the elderly as an alternative to institutional care. This shift is driven by the desire of older adults to remain in their homes, which is often more cost-effective and associated with a better quality of life. However, the relevance of this policy is questionable, as informal caregiving is on the decline—due to factors such as more women working, higher divorce rates, fewer children, and the growing trend of children living farther away. In light of these changes, consolidating elderly individuals in nursing homes may actually be a more sensible approach, both in terms of reducing costs and potentially improving quality of life.

A recent study by LaferrÃ¨re and Schoenmaeckers (2024), using SHARE data, suggests that while satisfaction among institutionalized individuals initially decreases after admission, it tends to return to pre-admission levels over time. This finding echoes earlier research by Bakx et al. (2020), which showed that delaying nursing home admission may not always result in better outcomes. Excess mortality in nursing homes is a critical issue in aging societies, particularly as the number of people over 80 is expected to double in the coming decades (OECD, 2020). However, there is limited evidence to suggest that spending the final years of life in a community setting accelerates death. The scarcity of administrative and survey data has hindered research in this area. Second, the choice between staying home with family help and going to nursing home is not trivial, particularly in case of pandemic such as COVID-19. In a recent paper covering a large number of countries and comparing the mortal impact of staying home versus residing in a nursing home, Flawinne et al. (2023) show that all things being constant staying home is safer in some countries (Germany, France, Eastern Europe) whereas in others it is safer to move to a nursing home.

A recent study by Bassoli et al. (2025) examines the case of France and finds that individuals living in nursing homes are no more likely to die than those residing at home, provided they have similar levels of limitations in activities of daily living (ADLs). Several other studies have sought to explore the mortality differences between people in nursing homes and those at home. For instance, Bakx et al. (2020) analyze administrative data from the Netherlands and conclude that mortality rates for nursing home residents are not significantly different from those for individuals living at home. Similarly, Braggion et al. (2020) use Italian data to show that mortality rates spike in the first few months after admission to a nursing home, particularly for patients who were recently hospitalized. In these cases, the deterioration of pre-existing chronic conditions is often the leading cause of death. In summary, while various studies have attempted to address the question of whether excess mortality occurs in nursing homes or at home, the evidence remains inconclusive.

These findings tend to suggest that home care may be preferable to institutional care, given its lower costs and additional benefits, particularly since mortality outcomes appear equivalent between the two settings.

3.2.7 Siblings' Location

As informal care becomes more intensive, it often demands geographical proximity, which can be challenging to reconcile with the career aspirations and mobility of adult children. The location of children can certainly be influenced by the need to care for aging or disabled parents, though it is not the sole determinant. A range of factors comes into play. When a parent requires significant care, children may opt to live closer to provide direct support. However, if professional caregivers or other family members are available, proximity may become less critical. Opportunities for higher wages or career advancement in distant locations might compel children to live farther away. The presence of other siblings or relatives who can assist with caregiving may also reduce the need for a child to relocate. Furthermore, cultural expectations can shape caregiving decisions: in some societies, there is an expectation for children to live near their aging parents, while in others, long-distance caregiving is more common. In essence, while geographical proximity can influence caregiving choices, it ultimately depends on the balance between direct (physical) and indirect (financial or logistical) support. When children live far from their aging parents due to professional or other commitments, their capacity for direct care is limited, often relegating them to a role focused on financial support.

Konrad et al. (2002) investigate whether the presence of younger siblings influences children's residential choices relative to their parents. Using a game-theoretic framework and data from the German Aging Survey, they show that birth order plays a significant role in caregiving decisions through strategic location choices. Specifically, they find that first-born children are more likely to live farther from their parents than second-born children or only children. This pioneering study introduces a novel perspective to the literature on intergenerational support, emphasizing the role of long-term strategic behavior within families. Hank (2007), using data from SHARE, identifies a striking North–South divide in Europe: while co-residence and daily contact are more prevalent in Mediterranean countries, Northern European families maintain frequent communication despite greater physical distance. He attributes these patterns to differing cultural norms and welfare systems, highlighting the importance of institutional context in shaping family dynamics. In contrast, Compton and Pollak (2013), using data from the National Survey of Families and Households (NSFH), find that, in the USA, proximity to elderly parents is driven more by children's education and marital status than by caregiving needs. They challenge the common assumption that proximity necessarily signals a caregiving intention and argue that co-residence and proximity should be treated as distinct behavioral choices.

Building on this idea, Johar and Maruyama (2012) show that siblings make location decisions non-cooperatively and proximate living with elderly parents is an under-provided public good. According to these authors, the impact of this public good problem is striking. Of the 2010 HRS families with multiple children, if families had fully internalized externality and jointly maximized family utility, 17% more parents would have had at least one child nearby. Maruyama and Johar (2017) conceptualize proximity as a strategic decision within families. Their sequential game-theoretic model suggests that siblings may deliberately avoid living close to elderly parents to shirk caregiving responsibilities, resulting in coordination failures. Using data from HRS, they find evidence of limited but notable strategic behavior. For example, in two-child families, over 92% of children exhibit dominant location strategies. They also find under-provision of informal care, largely due to free-riding. In families with three or more children, 28.8% make suboptimal location choices from the perspective of overall family welfare. Their analysis highlights a modest first-mover advantage and public goods inefficiencies—reporting that 18.3% more parents would have had at least one child living nearby under cooperative decision-making. Moreover, elder siblings may exploit early relocation as a strategic advantage. Given that informal care often substitutes for formal care when the latter is costly or limited, the authors argue that improved family coordination and targeted public policies—such as caregiver subsidies or location-based incentives—could enhance caregiving efficiency. Stern (2023) builds on the work of Konrad et al. (2002), Johar and Maruyama (2012) and Maruyama and Johar (2017), who focus on the strategic behavior of siblings with the result that a first-born child might have an incentive to move away, thus causing younger siblings to stay nearby. He extends this literature by modelling families with multiple children and adding uncertainty about the preferences of siblings among each other. Stern estimates the model using structural estimation methods to show that the addition of uncertainty plays an important role both in terms of model fit and in terms of welfare analysis.

Pezzin et al. (2009) explore another layer of family structure, showing that caregiving behavior varies depending on whether children are biological, joint, or stepchildren. Their findings underscore the importance of familial ties in shaping caregiving commitments within households. Engers and Stern (2002) introduce a structural game-theoretic model that allows for the possibility that not all family members engage in caregiving decisions—a departure from the collective decision-making assumptions often found in the literature. Using data from the 1984 National Long-Term Care Survey, they demonstrate that the voluntary participation model fits the data significantly better than the collective one. Their results indicate that distance from the parent is the strongest predictor of whether a child provides care, and that daughters and married children are more likely to do so. They also show that caregiving behavior responds to public subsidies, Medicaid policies, and the availability of formal care services. Extending this approach, Byrne et al. (2009) incorporate joint decision-making over caregiving, labor supply, consumption, and leisure into a comprehensive household model. Drawing on data from the Health and Retirement Study (AHEAD), they find that 22% of elderly respondents received some form of care, with 90% of these receiving informal (unpaid) care from family members. Caregiving is more likely among those with ADL (Activities of Daily Living) limitations, those who are unmarried, and women. They find evidence of strategic interactions, although these vary across family contexts. In a recent contribution, Nishimura et al. (2025) focus on the caregiving arrangements of two-sibling families, analyzing how their residential choices (close/close, far/far, or close/far) influence the levels of informal and formal care provided to a disabled parent. Key determinants include the nature of the relationship between siblings (cooperative vs. non-cooperative), the wage gap (affected by innate ability and location), the substitutability or complementarity between informal and formal care, the degree of altruism, the severity of the parent's disability, and the availability of public support.

3.2.8 Informal Versus Formal Care

As we see below, the relation between formal and informal care has an important impact on the design of public LTC policies. The relationship between informal and formal care is complex and can be both substitutive and complementary, depending on various factors. They are likely to be substitutes when informal caregivers provide services that would otherwise require paid formal care, when families choose between hiring professional help or providing care themselves or when policy frameworks treat them as alternatives (e.g., cash-for-care programs that allow beneficiaries to choose between formal services or paying family caregivers). On the contrary, they tend to be complementary when formal services support informal caregivers (respite care, training programs) or when formal care addresses specific medical needs while informal care provides emotional support and help with daily activities. Existing scanty literature suggests that the relationship depends on needs and intensity (higher dependency often requires both types) and on type of services (personal care vs. household help). Most evidence points to a mixed relationship where they can be both substitutes and complements depending on the specific circumstances and needs of the care recipient. Among early studies, we can mention Pezzin et al. (1996) who found evidence of substitution between informal and formal care in the USA, suggesting that formal care may crowd out family-provided care as well as Van Houtven and Norton (2004) who also concluded that formal and informal care are largely substitutes, using data from the U.S. Health and Retirement Survey (HRS).

In the European Context, we have the widely cited paper by Bonsang (2009) who examines the relationship between informal and formal care using data from

SHARE. It shows that informal care can substitute for formal care but primarily for low-skilled care needs. The substitution relationship depends significantly on the type of care and level of disability of the care recipient. Informal care tends to substitute for formal care when addressing low-skilled care needs (like household help or basic assistance with daily activities). As care needs become more complex and involve higher-skilled care (such as nursing or medical care), the relationship shifts toward complementarity rather than substitution. There is also the paper of Bolin et al. (2008) that examines substitution effects across European countries. In short, the existing literature provides mixed evidence, with context-specific and policy-contingent outcomes. While formal and informal care are often substitutes in terms of time and tasks, they may be complements in broader caregiving strategies, especially when informal caregivers provide emotional support and coordinate professional services.

Using the most recent waves of SHARE data, Perelman and Pestieau (2025) examine the complementarity and substitutability between formal and informal care across 27 European countries. The authors use data concerning the two types of care (formal m and informal a) for each disability level d. In the (a, m) plane, they obtain a point cloud corresponding to each value of d. From each cloud, they construct a best practice curve that identifies the optimal combinations of a and m for the considered disability level d. Their analysis reveals that these curves are concave and become increasingly curved as disability severity rises. This pattern demonstrates a nuanced relationship that depends critically on the level of disability: the elasticity of substitution between care types diminishes progressively with greater elderly dependency, indicating that formal and informal care become increasingly necessary rather than interchangeable as care needs intensify.

3.3 The State

The role of the state in providing long-term care (LTC) for older adults is becoming increasingly critical due to demographic shifts leading to aging populations in many countries. This importance is heightened by the negligible role of the market and the gradual retraction of traditional family caregiving roles. LTC encompasses a broad spectrum of services essential for individuals who cannot perform basic activities of daily living (ADLs), such as bathing, dressing, and eating, due to chronic illnesses, disabilities, or the natural aging process. One primary responsibility of the state is to ensure the funding and financial support for LTC. Typically, most nations maintain public programs specifically aimed at supporting low-income individuals, funded through taxation or social insurance systems. Moreover, states also offer direct financial assistance to individuals or subsidize services to enhance affordability. Equally crucial is the state's role in regulating LTC facilities to ensure quality care, safety, and the dignity of residents. This involves regular inspections and stringent enforcement of standards to uphold high-quality care.

Additionally, the state must implement training requirements for LTC staff to ensure they possess the necessary skills. This regulatory oversight is increasingly important given the rising incidents of abuse in institutions such as nursing homes. However, public intervention in LTC is often characterized by its underdevelopment and lack of coordination. Fragmentation within the system presents significant challenges, impacting the efficiency, quality, and overall accessibility of care. In many countries, the responsibility for LTC is scattered across various government levels—federal, regional, and local—leading to inconsistencies in policy, funding mechanisms, and service delivery models. This results in varied standards of care and eligibility criteria, creating disparities across regions.

Funding for LTC can originate from diverse sources, including public health insurance, social welfare programs, private insurance, and out-of-pocket payments. The complexity of these funding streams can complicate the navigation process for both service providers and recipients. There is a pronounced need for integrated care models. Some countries are advancing toward a more coordinated approach that aims to align healthcare, social services, and LTC. These efforts also include harmonizing policies across jurisdictions to establish a more uniform standard of care.

An example is France's Fifth Risk Plan, which seeks to address dependency in old age—a recognized "fifth risk" in its social protection scheme that already covers illness, old age, family, and employment. However, due to budget constraints, this initiative remains pending. By emphasizing greater coordination and integration, countries can strive for a more effective and equitable LTC system. This approach not only simplifies management and improves care quality but also ensures that the dignity and well-being of the elderly are sustainably protected. Two things seem certain. On one hand, the role of the State in long-term care will need to increase. On the other hand, the State must rely, as much as possible, on the two other pillars: family and the market. In the following chapter, we present a series of social insurance models that cover the loss of autonomy. It is impossible to capture every aspect of the interaction between the state, family, and market in a single model. Therefore, in the next section, we present models that focus on specific aspects of the relationship between public policy, family solidarity, and private insurance.

References

Achou, B. (2021). Housing liquidity and long-term care insurance demand: A quantitative evaluation. *Journal of Public Economics, 194*, Article 104353.

Alessie, R., Angelini, V., & Pasini, G. (2014). Is it true love? Altruism versus exchange in time and money transfers. *De Economist, 162*(2), 193–213.

Ameriks, J., Briggs, J., Caplin, A., Shapiro, M., & Tonetti, C. (2020). Long-term-care utility and late-in-life saving. *Journal of Political Economy, 128*, 2375–2451.

Angrisani, M., Lee, J., & Li, D. (2025). The mental health implications of informal care receipt stability, unpublished.

Arrow, K. (1963). Uncertainty and the welfare economics of medical care. *American Economic Review, 53*, 941–973.

Ayyagari, P., & He, D. (2019). Means-tested social insurance and strategic asset spend-down: Evidence from medicaid asset look-back policies. Working Paper. https://wmpeople.wm.edu/asset/index/dhe/assettransfer

Bakx, P., Wouterse, B., van Doorslaer, E., & Wong, A. (2020). Better off at home? Effects of nursing home eligibility on costs, hospitalizations and survival. *Journal of Health Economics, 73*, 102354. https://www.sciencedirect.com/science/article/pii/S0167629619307635

Basset, W. (2007). Medicaid's nursing home coverage and asset transfers. *Public Finance Review, 35*, 414–439.

Bassoli, B., Lefebvre, M., & Schoenmaeckers, J. (2025). Comparing health hutcomes in different care settings: Nursing homes vs. home care, unpublished.

Bernheim, B., Shleifer, A., & Summers, L. (1985). The strategic bequest motive. *Journal of Political Economy, 93*, 1045–1076.

Bolin, K., Lindgren, B., & Lundborg, P. (2008). Informal and formal care among single-living elderly in Europe. *Health Economics, 17*(3), 393–409.

Bonsang, E. (2009). Does informal care from children to their elderly parents substitute for formal care in Europe? *Journal of Health Economics, 28*, 143–154.

Boyer, M., De Donder, Ph., Fluet, C., Leroux M.-L. & Michaud P.-C. (2020). Long-Term Care Insurance: Information Frictions and Selection. *American Economic Journal: Economic Policy, 12*(3), 134–169.

Boyer, M., De Donder, P., Fluet, C., Leroux, M.-L., & Michaud, P.-C. (2019). Long-term care risk misperceptions. *The Geneva Papers on Risk and Insurance - Issues and Practice, 44*, 183–215.

Braggion, M., Pellizzari, M., Basso, C., Girardi, P., Zabeo, V., Lamattina, M.-R., Corti, M.-C., & Fedeli, U. (2020). Overall mortality and causes of death in newly admitted nursing home residents - Aging clinical and experimental research. https://link.springer.com/article/10.1007/s40520-019-01441-xciteas

Brenna, E., & Di Novi, C. (2016). Is caring for older parents detrimental to women's mental health? The role of the European North-South gradient. *Review of Economics of the Household, 14*, 745–778.

Brown, J., & Finkelstein, A. (2009). The private market for long-term care insurance in the U.S.: A review of the evidence. *Journal of Risk and Insurance, 76*(1), 5–29.

Brown, J., & Finkelstein, A. (2007). Why is the market for long-term care insurance so small? *Journal of Public Economics, 91*, 1967–1991.

Brown, J., & Finkelstein, A. (2008). The interaction of public and private insurance: Medicaid and the long-term care insurance market. *American Economic Review, 98*(3), 1083–1102.

Brown, J., & Warshawsky, M. (2013). The life care annuity: A new empirical examination of an insurance innovation that addresses problems in the markets for life annuities and long-term care insurance. *Journal of Risk and Insurance, 80*(3), 677–703.

Byrne, D., Goeree, M. S., Hiedemann, B., & Stern, S. (2009). Formal home health care, informal care, and family decision making. *International Economic Review, 50*(4), 1205–1242.

Canta, C., Pestieau, P., & Schoenmaeckers, J. (2024). Blood and gender bias in informal care within the family. *Review of Economics of the Household, 22*(2), 595–631.

Chaves Araujo, A., Pestieau, P., & Schoenmaeckers, J. (2025). Caring for disabled parents: Time or money? unpublished.

Chen, Y-P. (2001). Funding Long-term Care in the United States: The Role of Private Insurance, The Geneva Papers on Risk and Insurance. *Issues and Practice, 26,* 656–666.

Coe, N., Skira, M., & Larson, E. (2018). A comprehensive measure of the costs of caring for a parent: Differences according to functional status. *Health Policy and Economics, 66*, 2003–2008.

Coe, N., & Werner, R. (2022). Informal caregivers provide considerable front-line support in residential care facilities and nursing homes. *Health Affairs, 41*, 105–111.

Compton, J., & Pollak, R. (2013). Proximity and coresidence of adult children and their parents in the United States: Description and correlates. IZA Discussion Paper No. 7431.

Costa-Font, J., & Vilaplana-Prieto, C. (2024). The hidden value of adult informal care in Europe, IZA DP No. 17490.

Cremer, H. & Roeder, K. (2013). Long-term care policy, myopia and redistribution. *Journal of Public Economics, 108*, 33–43.

Cremer, H., Gahvari, F., & Pestieau, P. (2013). Endogenous altruism, redistribution, and long-term care. *The B.E. Journal of Economic Analysis & Policy, 14*(2), 499–524.

Cremer, H., Lozachmeur, J.-M., & Pestieau, P. (2016). The design of long-term care insurance contracts. *Journal of Health Economics, 50*, 330–339.

Davidoff, T. (2010). Home equity commitment and long-term care insurance demand. *Journal of Public Economics, 94*(1–2), 44–49.

De Donder, P., Leroux, M.-L., & Salani, F. (2022). Advantageous selection without moral hazard (with an application to life care annuities). TSE Working Paper, 1334.

De Donder, P., & Leroux, M.-L. (2013). Behavioral biases and long-term care insurance: A political economy approach. *The B.E. Journal of Economic Analysis & Policy, 14*, 551–575.

De Donder, P., & Leroux, M.-L. (2021). Long term care insurance with state-dependent preferences. *Health Economics, 30*, 3074–3086.

Dilnot, A. (2011). *Fairer care funding: The report of the commission on funding of care and support*. Commission on Funding of Care and Support.

Drèze, J., Pestieau, P., & Schokkaert, E. (2016). Arrow's theorem of the deductible and long-term care insurance. *Economics Letters, 148*, 103–105.

EC. (2021). Study on exploring the incidence and costs of informal long-term care in the EU, Brussels. https://op.europa.eu/en/publication-detail/-/publication/bafbb918-2197-11ec-bd8e-01aa75ed71a1/language-en

Engers, M., & Stern, S. (2002). Long-term care and family bargaining. *International Economic Review, 43*(1), 73–114.

Finkelstein, A., Luttmer, E., & Notowidigdo, M. (2013). What good is wealth without health? The effect of health on the marginal utility of consumption. *Journal of the European Economic Association, 11*(S1), 221–258.

Genworth CareScout. (2024). Cost of care trends and insights. https://www.carescout.com/cost-of-care

Hanewald, K., Eaton, R., & Long Ho, T. (2020). *The home stretch: Accessing home value to fund long-term care*. Long Term News: Society of Actuaries.

Hank, K. (2007). Spatial proximity and contacts between elderly parents and their adult children: A European comparison. *Journal of Marriage and Family, 69*(1), 157–173.

Hiedemann, B., & Stern, S. (1999). Strategic play among family members when making long-term care decisions. *Journal of Economic Behavior & Organization, 40*, 29–57.

Ho, C., & McGarry, K. (2025). Brothers, sisters, and support to older parents: Separate spheres across and within support types? *Journal of Population Economics, 38*, 25.

Johar, M., & Maruyama, S. (2012). Externality and Strategic Interaction in the Location Choice of Siblings under Altruism toward Parents, Working Paper 201201, ARC Centre of Excellence in Population Ageing Research (CEPAR), Australian School of Business, University of New South Wales.

Kaschowitz, J., & Brandt, M. (2017). Health effects of informal caregiving across Europe: A longitudinal approach. *Social Science & Medicine, 173*, 72–80.

Kim, G. (2018). Medicaid crowd-out of long-term care insurance with endogenous Medicaid enrollment. *Journal of Human Capital, 12*, 431–474.

Klimaviciute, J., & Pestieau, P. (2020). Insurance with a deductible: a way out of the long term care insurance puzzle. *Journal of Economics, 130*, 297–307.

Klimaviciute, J., Perelman, S., Pestieau, P., & Schoenmaeckers, J. (2017). Caring for dependent parents: altruism, exchange or family norm? *Journal of Population Economics, 30*, 835–873.

Klimaviciute, J., Pestieau, P. & Schoenmaeckers, J. (2020). Long-Term Care Insurance With Family Altruism: Theory and Empirics. *Journal of Risk and Insurance, 87*, 895–918.

Klimaviciute, J. (2017). Long-term care insurance and intra-family moral hazard: Fixed vs proportional insurance benefits. *The Geneva Risk and Insurance Review, 42*, 87–116.

Klimaviciute, J. (2019). Long-term care and intra-family moral hazard: Optimal public policy. *Journal of Public Economic Theory, 21*, 1037–1055.
Klimaviciute, J. (2020). Long-term care and myopic couples. *International Tax and Public Finance, 27*, 77–102.
Klimaviciute, J., & Pestieau, P. (2018a). Long-term care social insurance: How to avoid big losses? *International Tax and Public Finance,25*, 99–139.
Klimaviciute, J., & Pestieau, P. (2018b). Social insurance for long-term care with deductible and linear contributions. *FinanzArchiv,74*, 88–108.
Koijen, R., Van Nieuwerburgh, S., & Yogo, M. (2016). Health and mortality delta: Assessing the welfare cost of household insurance choice. *Journal of Finance, 71*(2), 957–1010.
Konrad, K., & Künemund, H., Lommerud, K., Kjell, E., & Robledo, J. (2002). Geography of the family. *American Economic Review, 92*, 981–998.
Kopczuk, W., & Slemrod, J. (2005). Denial of death and economic behavior. *The B.E. Journal of Theoretical Economics, 5*.
Kotlikoff, L., & Morris, J. (1990). Why don't the elderly live with their children? A new look. In W. David (Ed.), *Issues in the economics of aging*. University of Chicago Press.
Laferrère, A., & Schoenmaeckers, J. (2024). Do Europeans really feel better at home than in a nursing home?. *American Journal of Epidemiology, 87*.
Lefèbvre, M., Pestieau, P. & Schoenmaeckers, J. (2025), Childcare and eldercare. A quid pro quo compact, Economic Modelling, forthcoming.
Lillard, L., & Weiss, Y. (1997). Uncertain health and survival: Effects on end-of-life consumption. *Journal of Business & Economic Statistics, 15*(2), 254–268.
Liu, J., & Mukherjee, A. (2020). Medicaid and long-term care: The effects of penalizing strategic asset transfers. *The Journal of Risk and Insurance*.
Lozachmeur, J.-M., Pestieau, P., & Schoenmackers, J. (2025). Spending down for needs-based LTC programs, unpublished.
Maruyama, S., & Johar, M. (2017). Do siblings free-ride in "being there" for parents? *Quantitative Economics, 8*(1), 277–316.
Murtaugh, C., Spillman, B., & Warshawsky, M. (2001). In sickness and in health: An annuity approach to financing long-term care and retirement income. *Journal of Risk and Insurance, 68*(2), 225–254.
Nishimura, Y., Pestieau, P., Schoenmakers, J., & Theodoropoulos, N. (2025). Siblings caring for their parents either in time or in money, unpublished.
Nordman, E. (2016). The state of long-term care insurance: The market, challenges and future innovations. NAIC and Center for Insurance Policy and Research.
Norton, E. (1995). Elderly assets, Medicaid policy, and spend-down in nursing homes. *Review of Income and Wealth, 41*(3), 309–329.
OECD. (2020). Long-term care and health care insurance in OECD and other countries. www.oecd.org/fin/insurance/Long-Term-Care-Health-Care-Insurance-in-OECD-and-Other-Countries.htm
Pauly, M. V. (1990). The rational non-purchase of long term care insurance. *Journal of Political Economy, 98*, 153–168.
Perelman, P., & Pestieau, P. (2025). Informal and formal care for disabled elderly individuals. Substitutes or complements? unpublished.
Pestieau, P., & Ponthière, G. (2012). The long term care insurance puzzle. In J. Costa-Font & C. Courbage (Eds.), *Financing long term care in Europe: Institutions* (pp. 41–52). Markets and Models: Palgrave Macmillan.
Pezzin, L., Kemper, P., & Reschovsky, J. (1996). Does publicly provided home care substitute for family care?: Experimental evidence with endogenous living arrangements. *Journal of Human Resources, 31*(3).
Pezzin, L., Pollak, R., & Schone, B. (2009). Long-term care of the disabled elderly: Do children increase caregiving by spouses? *Review of Economics of the Household, 7*, 323–339.

Schneider, U., & Kleindienst, J. (2016). Monetising the provision of informal long-term care by elderly people: Estimates for European out-of-home caregivers based on the well-being valuation method. *Health & Social Care in the Community, 24*(5), e81–e91.
Schulz, R., & Sherwood, P. R. (2008). Physical and mental health effects of family caregiving. *American Journal of Nursing, 108*, 23–27.
Sloan, F., & Norton, E. (1997). Adverse selection, bequests, crowding out, and private demand for insurance: Evidence from the long-term care insurance market. *Journal of Risk and Uncertainty, 15*, 201–219.
Stern, S. (2023). Where have all my siblings gone? *Journal of Human Resources, 53*, 852–891.
Stöckel, J., & Bom, J. (2022). Revisiting longer-term health effects of informal caregiving: Evidence from the UK. *The Journal of the Economics of Aging, 21*.
Trainar, P. (2024). Le marché de l'assurance dépendance. *Revue d'économie financière, 0*(4), 151–165.
Van Houtven, C., Coe, N., & Skira, M. (2013). The effect of informal care on work and wages. *Journal of Health Economics, 32*, 240–252.
Van Houtven, C., & Norton, E. (2004). Informal care and health care use of older adults. *Journal of Health Economics, 23*(6), 1159–80.
Venti, S. F., & Wise, D. A. (2004). Aging and housing equity: Another look. In *Perspectives on the economics of aging* (pp. 127–180).
Vlachantoni, A., Evandrou, M., Falkingham, J., & Robards, J. (2013). Informal care, health and mortality. *Maturitas, 74*(2), 114–118.
Wiener, J., Anderson, W., Khatutsky, G., Kaganova, Y., & O'Keeffe, J. (2013). *Medicaid spend down: New estimates and implications for long-term services and supports financing reform.* The SCAN Foundation.
Wiener, J., Romaire, M., Thach, N., Collins, A., Kim, K., Pan, H., Chiri, G., Sommers, A., Haber, S., Musumeci, M., & Paradise, J. (2017). Strategies to reduce Medicaid spending: Findings from a literature review. https://www.kff.org/medicaid/issue-brief/strategies-to-reduce-medicaid-spending-findings-from-a-literature-review/view/print/
Zhou-Richter, T., Browne, M., & Gründl, H. (2010). Don't they care? Or, are they just unaware? Risk perception and the demand for long-term care insurance. *Journal of Risk and Insurance, 77*(4), 715–747.
Zweifel P. & Courbage, Ch. (2016). Long-term care: is there crowding out of informal care private insurance as well as saving? *Asia-Pacific Journal of risk and Insurance, De Gruyter, 10*(1), 107–132.
Zweifel, P., & Strüwe, W. (1998). Long-term care insurance in a two-generation model. *Journal of Risk and Insurance, 65*(1), 13–32.

Chapter 4
Models of Social Insurance

In this chapter, we explore various models of public long-term care (LTC) insurance schemes. Our analysis begins by excluding the role of family—spouse and children—in providing care. We then incorporate family assistance, focusing particularly on support from children. Unlike previous chapters, this one adopts a more analytical approach. Below, we present a concise summary of the key points covered in each section.

When family solidarity is set aside, the optimal solution for long-term care would not necessitate social insurance. In this framework, a combination of non-distortionary income taxation and actuarially fair private insurance would suffice. However, when tax distortions are inevitable, social LTC insurance becomes beneficial—especially under the widely accepted assumption that disability risk and income are negatively correlated. Social insurance, in this case, facilitates a more efficient redistribution of resources with fewer distortions compared to income taxation.

When family support is considered, it becomes essential to distinguish between situations where such care is guaranteed and those where it is uncertain. Practical constraints, such as labor mobility or health issues, can render eldercare by children or spouses impractical, and these factors must be accounted for in designing LTC social insurance. For example, in cases where filial altruism varies but income is uniform, social insurance should primarily support elderly individuals who cannot depend on their children. Conversely, when altruism is unobservable, public benefits are typically kept modest to prevent exploitation by altruistic families. The interaction between private insurance and the conditional nature of public benefits further shapes the desirability of social LTC insurance.

Disability often reduces the value of bequests, as children of healthy parents inherit more than those whose parents face prolonged, expensive periods of disability. This dynamics suggests that taxing bequests could serve as a practical method for funding public LTC benefits. Moreover, in scenarios where mutual altruism exists between

P. Pestieau, *The Economics of Long-term Care*, Developments in Health Economics and Public Policy 14, https://doi.org/10.1007/978-3-032-18237-1_4

parents and children, a strong case can be made for integrating social LTC insurance with an inheritance tax and subsidies for informal care.

One factor contributing to the limited uptake of LTC insurance is the unattractive reimbursement structures typically offered. The market often struggles to adequately cover individuals who experience extended periods of dependency. To address this, a deductible system has been proposed. Under such a scheme, individuals would bear a portion of their dependency costs for a defined period, after which all expenses exceeding a certain threshold would be covered by social insurance. Public intervention becomes even more necessary when governments are more efficient than private insurers or when LTC needs vary significantly across individuals.

In many countries, access to social assistance for dependency care is subject to means testing. However, it is often observed that individuals who initially have sufficient resources to cover their own needs deliberately impoverish themselves to qualify for benefits that are not intended for them. This raises the question of how such behavior can be effectively prevented.

Most of the models discussed in this analysis are static in nature. However, we also present a dynamic approach that examines the impact of dependency on capital accumulation and national production, as well as the potential effects of public insurance on these variables. The findings suggest that dependency tends to stimulate capital accumulation, whereas public insurance has a discouraging effect on it.

Most LTC social insurance models are normative, grounded in a utilitarian framework. However, adopting alternative objectives—such as ex post egalitarianism—can lead to markedly different conclusions. Positive models that examine the political economy of LTC, while less common than those focusing on optimal policy design, offer valuable insights into the political feasibility of public schemes. These models often uncover some degree of political support for social LTC programs, although such support may be undermined by factors like family solidarity, behavioral biases, or the availability of more actuarially fair private insurance.

This chapter takes an analytical approach, distinguishing it from the preceding chapters. We present several normative models of social long-term care (LTC) insurance, each designed to identify optimal policy instruments—taxes, subsidies, and benefits—that maximize a utilitarian welfare function while accounting for individual behavioral responses. Our modeling framework adopts a Stackelberg strategic game structure in which the state serves as the leader, making initial policy decisions, while families respond sequentially as followers. We employ either linear or non-linear policy instruments depending on the specific case under examination. The framework operates under conditions of asymmetric information. Following standard assumptions in the literature, the government cannot observe individual characteristics such as survival probability, dependency risk, or labor productivity when designing policy. Instead, it must rely on observable actions including earnings, saving behavior, insurance purchases, public benefit claims, and care provision levels. This information constraint places the analysis in a second-best setting, contrasting with the first-best scenario where the government would possess complete information about individual characteristics and choices. The chapter ends with a comprehensive list of notations used throughout the analysis.

4.1 Social Insurance Without the Family

We first present a model demonstrating that social insurance might be desirable for redistributive purposes even when income taxation is available.[1] The reason is that under some plausible assumptions, social insurance does not entail distortions while redistributive income taxation does.

4.1.1 Individual's Problem

Consider a two-period model, where individuals work and save in the first period. Individuals are distinguished according to three characteristics: wage (earning ability) w_i, the probability to be alive in the second period, ϕ_i, and the probability π_i of becoming disabled in the second period. An individual of type i has a lifetime expected utility given by

$$U_i = u(c_i - v(l_i)) + (1 - \phi_i)\pi_i u(d_i) + \phi_i \pi_i H(m_i)$$

where c_i denotes the first-period consumption; d_i represents the second-period consumption if healthy, while m_i denotes LTC expenditures in case of dependence. The disutility of labor l_i is given by the convex function $v(l_i)$. The utility functions $u(.)$ and $H(.)$ are assumed to be strictly concave with $u(z) > H(z)$. This latter inequality implies that more resources are needed so as the disabled reach the same level of utility as the healthy elderly. Throughout most of this chapter, we assume zero interest rate and no time preference without loss of generality. Earnings in the first period is devoted to consumption, saving, and LTC insurance premium. We assume quasi linearity of the disutility of labor, such that net consumption is equal to $x_i = c_i - v(l_i)$. Private saving, s_i, is invested in a perfect annuity market so that we have $d_i = s_i/\phi_i$. Assuming no loading cost, an insurance premium I_i yields a benefit $I_i/\phi_i\pi_i$ to the disabled elderly, whose LTC spending thus amounts to $m_i = s_i/\phi_i + I_i/\phi_i\pi_i$. We can now write the lifetime utility to be maximized as:

$$U_i = u(w_i l_i - s_i - I_i - v(l_i)) + (1 - \phi_i)\,\pi_i u(s_i/\phi_i + I_i/\pi_i\phi_i) \\ + \phi_i \pi_i H(s_i/\phi_i + I_i/\pi_i\phi_i)$$

Assuming interior solutions, the FOCs are:

$$v'(l_i) = w_i;\, u'(x_i) = u'(d_i) = H'(m_i)$$

[1] See Rochet (1991), Cremer and Pestieau (1996, 2014).

At this point, a remark on the function $H(m)$ is in order. We assume that a dependent individual essentially consumes "care" and that his utility function is state dependent. Implicitly, we assume a state of severe dependence due to a cognitive impairment (like Alzheimer's disease) that in general leads to institutionalization. We realize that in a state of light dependence, it would make sense to have a utility function with two arguments, standard consumption and care, like it is usual in health economics. In those models, the substitutability between the two arguments is a crucial matter. Ideally, we would like to introduce different levels and types of dependency. We do that below.

4.1.2 Social LTC Benefits

With the linear tax specification adopted here, we have three instruments: a (uniform) social LTC benefit, g, a demogrant[2] T and a proportional tax on wage income at rate τ. We thus have:

$$U_i = u(w_i l_i (1-\tau) + T - s_i - I_i - v(l_i)) + (1-\phi_i)\pi_i u(s_i/\phi_i + I_i/\pi_i\phi_i)$$

$$+ \phi_i \pi_i H(s_i/\phi_i + I_i/\pi_i\phi_i + g),$$

where the subscript i denotes the type of individuals that are characterized by the triplets (w_i, π_i, ϕ_i). The relative number of individuals of type i is given by n_i. We can then write the revenue constraint of the government:

$$\sum n_i (\pi_i \phi_i g - \tau w_i l_i) + T = 0.$$

There are two types of insurance: private (actuarially fair) and social (redistributive). Given risk aversion and actuarial fairness,[3] there will be full insurance. The question is whether it is to be provided by the government or the market. We can now write the problem of the social planner using the operator E so that $Ez = \sum n_i z_i$. It amounts to maximize the following Lagrangian:

$$\mathcal{L} = E[U - \mu(T + \pi\phi g - \tau w l)]$$

where μ is the multiplier associated with the revenue constraint.

Using the envelope theorem and assuming again interior solutions except for g, we have:

---

[2] lump-sum transfer.

[3] This is a simplifying assumption as the loadings of private LTC insurance are actually substantial.

$$\frac{\partial \mathcal{L}}{\partial T} = Eu'(x) - \mu = 0 \tag{4.1}$$

$$\frac{\partial \mathcal{L}}{\partial \tau} = E\left[-u'(x)wl + \mu\left(wl - \tau w\frac{\partial l}{\partial \tau}\right)\right] = 0 \tag{4.2}$$

$$\frac{\partial \mathcal{L}}{\partial g} = EH'(m)\pi\phi - \mu E\pi\phi \tag{4.3}$$

Combining, (4.1) and (4.3), we obtain:

$$\frac{\partial \mathcal{L}}{\partial g} = Eu'(x)\pi\phi - Eu'(x)E\pi\phi = cov\left(u'(x), \pi\phi\right) \tag{4.4}$$

According to Eq. (4.4), $\frac{\partial \mathcal{L}}{\partial g} > 0$ as long as the covariance between $u'(x)$ and $\pi\phi$ is positive. This is indeed the case as we know that x is positively correlated with w and we learn from Lefèbvre et al. (2025) that the probability of being dependent decreases with income.

Combining the FOCs (4.1) and (4.2), we obtain the compensated effect of the tax on welfare:

$$\frac{\partial \mathcal{L}}{\partial \tau} + \frac{\partial \mathcal{L}}{\partial T}Ewl = -E\left[u'(x)wl\right] + Eu'(x)Ewl + \mu\tau Ew\frac{\partial l}{\partial \tau} = 0,$$

where $\frac{dT}{d\tau} = Ewl$ denotes the amount of lump sum transfer obtained from an increase in taxation.

This can be rewritten as:

$$\tau = \frac{-cov(u'(x), wl)}{-\mu Ew\frac{\partial l}{\partial \tau}} > 0, \tag{4.5}$$

where $\frac{\partial l}{\partial \tau} < 0$ denotes the effect of the tax on the labor supply. This effect is negative. The numerator of the tax formula (4.4) represents the equity effect of the tax $\left(cov(u'(x), wl) < 0\right)$. The size of the equity effect depends on the wage inequality and on the concavity of the utility function. As to the denominator, it reflects the efficiency effect. If the labor supply is inelastic, in other words, if the tax does not much modify the individual behavior, the tax will tend to be high. This result rests on the assumption of an interior solution for I_i. This assumption is not necessarily met. We can expect that if g is generous enough, low-income individuals would not purchase LTC insurance.

4.1.3 Extensions

We now turn to a number of extensions of this basic model.

4.1.3.1 Myopia and Loading Costs

In the above model, disability risk was assumed to be correctly perceived. As we saw in the section devoted to the LTC insurance puzzle, there is some evidence that this is far from being the case. In that respect, Cremer and Roeder (2013)[4] examine scenarios where individuals underestimate their future disability needs. They model individual differences in productivity, survival probability, disability risk, and awareness of these risks. While productivity is positively correlated with survival rates and negatively with dependency, the net probability of becoming dependent doesn't necessarily decrease with higher productivity. In optimal scenarios, subsidizing private LTC insurance or implementing social insurance could mitigate these issues. The choice depends on the actuarial fairness of private insurance; unfair private markets make a stronger case for social insurance, which, however, can be regressively distributed and thus less effective in non-ideal conditions.

4.1.3.2 Pensions Versus LTC Benefits

Thus far, the pension dimension has been overlooked. Yet pensions and LTC benefits represent the two principal public programs targeting the elderly, and they often compete for limited public resources. We thus now extend the above model by introducing public pensions, keeping two types of uncertainty pertaining to mortality and disability. Individuals are distinguished by their productivity, w_i, their survival probability, ϕ_i, and their disability risk, π_i. We consider a government that has to adopt two public policies: a LTC benefit as above and a flat rate pension P. To study such a choice, we adapt the above model by modifying the revenue constraint:

$$E\left[\pi\phi g + \phi P + T - \tau w l\right] = 0.$$

and the individual utility:

$$U_i = u(w_i l_i\,(1-\tau) + T - s_i - I_i - v(l_i)) + \phi_i(1-\pi_i)u(s_i/\phi_i + I_i/\pi_i\phi_i + P)$$
$$+\,\phi_i\pi_i H(s_i/\phi_i + I_i/\pi_i\phi_i + g + P)$$

Assuming interior solutions, we have: $u'(x_i) = u'(d_i) = H'(m_i)$.

---

[4] See also Cremer and Roeder (2017).

The problem for the government is thus to find the policy tools that maximize the following Lagrangian:

$$\mathcal{L} = E\left[U - \mu\left(T + \pi\phi g + \phi P - \tau wl\right)\right]$$

Focusing on the FOCs with respect to the LTC benefits and the pension level,[5] we have:

$$\frac{\partial \mathcal{L}}{\partial g} = EH'(m)\pi\phi - \mu E\pi\phi \tag{4.6}$$

$$\frac{\partial \mathcal{L}}{\partial P} = E\left[u'(d)\phi(1-\pi) + H'(m)\pi\phi\right] - \mu E\phi \tag{4.7}$$

Combining (4.6) and (4.7), we obtain the effect of increasing public LTC spending at the expense of public pension on social welfare:

$$\frac{\partial \mathcal{L}}{\partial g} + \frac{\partial \mathcal{L}}{\partial P}\frac{E\pi\phi}{E\phi} = \frac{E\phi(1-\pi)}{E\phi}cov\left(u', \pi\phi\right) - \frac{E\pi\phi}{E\phi}cov\left(u', \phi(1-\pi)\right) > 0$$

The inequality sign comes from Lefèbvre et al. (2025) who show that there is a negative correlation between income and the risk of dependence and a positive one between income and the probability of being healthy in old age.

Nishimura and Pestieau (2022) delve into these comparative merits of social insurance for long-term care versus public pension systems in departing from the above interior solutions assumption that implies the possibility for the poor households to borrow against future social benefits. Their findings suggest that a utilitarian government would prioritize LTC insurance due to its broad societal benefits, whereas a Rawlsian government's decision would hinge on the relative metrics of survival versus dependence risk among the less affluent compared to the population average.

Despite this finding, we observe a pronounced political preference for public pensions over long-term care insurance. This preference stems from several interconnected factors embedded in electoral dynamics, institutional frameworks, and economic incentives. Pensions command broad political support because they benefit virtually all elderly citizens, while long-term care serves a smaller, more vulnerable population. Additionally, family support networks tend to be more robust for disabled parents than for healthy ones, further influencing policy priorities.

4.1.3.3 Types of Disability

LTC economists tend to consider dependence as a one-dimensional reality, whose only variability would be its severity. One would be more or less seriously dependent. In reality, there are different sources of old age dependence. Among these sources,

[5] We implicitly assume that $T = 0$..

one can cite age-related disabilities from chronic diseases such as pulmonary disease and diabetes, age-related loss of hearing, sight, and movement (arthritis), cognitive illnesses such as dementia and Alzheimer.

It is important to take into account this heterogeneity in the causes of dependence for two reasons. Health care and nursing can vary from one type to another. And social policy can also vary from one type to another. Using SHARE data, one can distinguish between forms of dependency and show how each of them is differently distributed across the income scale. On that basis, we develop a theoretical model of LTC social insurance that takes this distinction into account. Unlike the previous subsection, this model follows the non-linear approach of Atkinson and Stiglitz (1976).

We consider a society comprising two types of individuals, denoted $i = 1, 2$ where each type is characterized by three parameters: productivity w_i, the probability π_{1i} of incurring a disability of category 1 that increases with w_i and the probability π_{2i} of incurring a disability of category 2 that is negatively correlated with w_i. We assume that $w_1 < w_2$. There is no uncertainty over the lifetime.

Individual utility is given by:

$$U_i = u(c_i) - v(l_i) + (1 - \pi_{1i} - \pi_{2i})\, u(d_i) + \pi_{1i} H(m_{1i}) + \pi_{2i} V(m_{2i})$$

where c_i and d_i denote consumption in first and second period when healthy; l_i is labor supply. The variables m_{1i} and m_{2i} denote the long-term care needed in case of disability 1 and 2. The utility functions $u(.)$, $V(.)$, $H(.)$ are strictly concave and $v(.)$ strictly convex. We assume that both retirement and disability can be financed with actuarially fair insurance products. We posit that the social planner can observe earnings $y_i = w_i l_i$, consumption spending d_i and LTC spending m_{1i} and m_{2i}. We write the lifetime utility function as:

$$U_i = u[y_i - \theta_y(y_i) - (1 - \pi_{1i} - \pi_{2i})\,(d_i + \theta_d(d_i))) - \pi_{1i}\,(m_{1i} + \theta_{1i}(m_{1i}))$$

$$- \pi_{2i}\,(m_{2i} + \theta_{2i}(m_{2i}))] + (1 - \pi_{1i} - \pi_{2i})\, u(d_i) + \pi_{1i} H(m_{1i}) + \pi_{2i} V(m_{2i}) - v(y_i/w_i)$$

where the functions $\theta_z(z_i)$ denote the non-linear tax (or subsidy) on z_i with $z_i = y_i, d_i, m_{1i}, m_{2i}$.

From the FOCs for the individual utility maximization, we obtain the following rates of substitution that may include some distortions.

$$\frac{v'(l_i)}{u'(c_i)} = w_i(1 - \theta_y'(y_i))$$

$$\frac{u'(d_i)}{u'(c_i)} = 1 + \theta_d'(d_i)$$

$$\frac{H'(m_{1i})}{u'(c_i)} = 1 + \theta'_{1i}(m_{1i})$$

$$\frac{V'(m_{2i})}{u'(c_i)} = 1 + \theta'_{2i}(m_{2i})$$

In these expressions, $\theta'_z(z_i)$ denotes the marginal tax on $z_i = y_i, d_i, m_{1i}, m_{2i}$.

We want to maximize the utilitarian social welfare $\sum n_i U_i$ subject to the resource constraint:

$$\sum n_i \left[c_i + (1 - \pi_{1i} - \pi_{2i})\, d_i + \pi_{1i} m_{1i} + \pi_{2i} m_{2i} - y_i\right] = 0,$$

where n_i denotes the relative number of type i's individuals.

We assume that individuals of type 2 will be tempted to mimic individuals of type 1 so that we have the following self-selection constraint:

$$u(c_2) - v(y_2/w_2) + (1 - \pi_{12} - \pi_{22})\, u(d_2) + \pi_{12} H(m_{12}) + \pi_{22} V(m_{2H})$$

$$- u(c_1) + v(y_1/w_2) - (1 - \pi_{12} - \pi_{22})\, u(d_1) - \pi_{12} H(m_{11}) + \pi_{22} V(m_{21}) = 0.$$

Denoting μ, the multiplier associated with the resource constraint and λ, the multiplier associated with the self-selection constraint, we write the Lagrangian expression to be maximized by the social planner as:

$$\mathcal{L} = \sum n_i \left[u(x_i) - v(y_i/w_i) + (1 - \pi_{1i} - \pi_{2i})\, u(d_i) + \pi_{1i} H(m_{1i}) + \pi_{2i} V(m_{2i})\right]$$

$$- \mu \sum n_i \left(c_i + (1 - \pi_{1i} - \pi_{2i})\, d_i + \pi_{1i} m_{1i} + \pi_{2i} m_{2i} - y_i\right)$$

$$+ \lambda \left[U_2 - u(c_1) + v(y_1/w_2) - (1 - \pi_{12} - \pi_{22})\, u(d_1) - \pi_{12} H(m_{11}) + \pi_{22} V(m_{21})\right]$$

The FOCs are given by:

$$u'(c_2)\,[n_2 + \lambda] - \mu n_2 = 0$$

$$u'(d_2)\,[n_2 + \lambda] - \mu n_2 = 0$$

$$H'(m_{12})\,[n_2 + \lambda] - \mu n_2 = 0$$

$$V'(m_{22})\,[n_2 + \lambda] - \mu n_2 = 0$$

$$- v'(y_2/w_2)\,[n_2 + \lambda] + \mu n_2 w_2 = 0$$

$$\left[u'(c_1)-\mu\right]n_1-\lambda u'(c_1)=0$$

$$\left[u'(d_1)-\mu\right]n_1-\lambda\frac{1-\pi_{12}-\pi_{22}}{1-\pi_{11}-\pi_{21}}u'(d_1)=0$$

$$\left[H'(m_{11})-\mu\right]n_1-\lambda\frac{\pi_{12}}{\pi_{11}}H'(m_{11})=0$$

$$\left[V'(m_{21})-\mu\right]n_1-\lambda\frac{\pi_{22}}{\pi_{21}}V'(m_{21})=0$$

$$-\left[\frac{v'(y_1/w_1)}{w_1}-\mu\right]n_1+\lambda\frac{v'(y_1/w_2)}{w_2}=0$$

From the first five FOCs, one easily gets the no distortion at the top result:

$$u'(c_2)=\frac{v'(y_2/w_2)}{w_2}=u'(d_2)=H'(m_{12})=V'(m_{22})=\frac{\mu n_2}{n_2+\lambda}$$

As to the type 1's individuals, we can rewrite their FOCs as follows:

$$\frac{u'(d_1)}{u'(c_1)}=\frac{n_1-\lambda}{n_1-\lambda\frac{1-\pi_{12}-\pi_{22}}{1-\pi_{11}-\pi_{21}}}=1+\theta_d^{'}(d_1)>1 \tag{4.8}$$

$$\frac{H'(m_{11})}{u'(c_1)}=\frac{n_1-\lambda}{n_1-\lambda\frac{\pi_{12}}{\pi_{11}}}=1+\theta_{11}^{'}(m_{11})>1 \tag{4.9}$$

$$\frac{V'(m_{21})}{u'(c_1)}=\frac{n_1-\lambda}{n_1-\lambda\frac{\pi_{22}}{\pi_{21}}}1+\theta_{21}^{'}(m_{21})<1 \tag{4.10}$$

$$\frac{v'(y_1/w_1)}{u'(c_1)w_1}=1+\frac{\lambda}{\mu n_1}\left[\frac{v'(y_1/w_2)}{w_2}-\frac{v'(y_1/w_1)}{w_1}\right]=1-\theta_y^{'}(y_1)<1 \tag{4.11}$$

We signed the equations so that we have a tax on d_1 and on m_{11}, a subsidy on m_{21} and a tax on y_1. The tax on d_1 and on m_{11} can be explained by the assumption that the rich live longer in good health and suffer from type 1 dependence more than the poor. The subsidy on m_{21} comes from the fact that $\pi_{22}<\pi_{21}$. Finally, the tax on labor is standard.

4.1.3.4 Social Criterion

The literature on long-term care (LTC) public policy predominantly adopts a utilitarian framework, whereby the social planner seeks to maximize the sum of individual expected utilities. Recently, scholars have challenged this approach, arguing for compensation to those who become disabled through no fault of their own.[6] A key limitation of utilitarianism emerges when examining lifetime uncertainty. Consider two individuals, each with identical initial endowment w, but differing lifespans: one lives for a single period, the other for two periods. Assuming a zero interest rate and no time preference, the utilitarian planner aims at maximizing the sum of lifetime utilities, represented as:

$$u(c_1) + u(d_1) + u(c_2)$$

subject to the resource constraint $c_1 + d_1 + c_2 = 2w$, where c_i and d_i denote first and second-period consumption, respectively.

The utilitarian solution reveals that $c_1 = d_1 = c_2 = 2w/3$. This results in the first individual receiving twice as much consumption as the second individual. This outcome highlights a critical flaw: the utilitarian approach fails to account for fairness in distribution when lifetimes differ. Formally, with the ex post approach, the allocation of consumption levels is determined by the equation:

$$u(c_1) + u(d_1) = u(c_2)$$

that implies $c_2 > c_1 = d_1$.

Turning to the issue of disability in old age, if one adopts the utilitarian criterion, the disabled elderly should receive more resources than the autonomous elderly, since the former exhibits a higher capacity to convert resources into well-being, granted that $u'(z) < H'(z)$. However, this does not insure that this will compensate for the disability. On the contrary, under the ex post egalitarian social criterion, more resources should be allocated to the dependent elderly than to the autonomous elderly, so as to compensate him/her for dependency. The postulated normative criterion has also crucial consequences for the overall shape of consumption profiles.

To emphasize the difference between the two approaches, we will take the case where the marginal utility of the disabled elderly is lower than that of the healthy elderly.

Assume identical individuals with utility for consumption $u(c)$ and $u(d)$ and utility for LTC $H(m)$, both being strictly concave, fulfilling Inada conditions and such that

$$u(x) > H(x); u'(x) > H'(m)$$

---

[6] Leroux et al. (2021).

The lifetime expected utility of the individual is

$$U = u(w - s - I) + (1 - \pi)\, u(s) + \pi\, H(s + I/\pi),$$

where we assume a zero interest rate.

The FOCs are given by

$$\frac{\partial U}{\partial s} = -u'(c) + \big(1 - \pi)u'(s\big) + \pi\, H'(s + I/\pi) \tag{4.12}$$

$$\frac{\partial U}{\partial I} = -u'(c) + H'(s + I/\pi) \tag{4.13}$$

Given our assumptions, (4.12) is binding and (4.13) is not. This means that not only the individuals will not purchase an actuarially fair insurance but that a utilitarian government will not provide such an insurance.

Let us now assume that the government wants to achieve an ex post equality between the utilities of the healthy elderly and that of the disabled elderly. It is clear that such equality is not obtained in the laissez faire since:

$$U^H = u(w - s) + u(s) > U^D = u(w - s) + H(s)$$

To do so, it is going to provide a LTC benefit g such that:

$$H(s + g) = u(s) \tag{4.14}$$

where $\tau = \pi g$ is a tax levied ex ante in the first period. The problem of the individual ex ante is to find the value of s that maximizes:

$$U = u(w - s - \tau) + (1 - \pi)\, u(s) + \pi\, H(s + g)$$

The FOC is the same as (4.12). Combining (4.12) and (4.14), we get a positive value for the public LTC benefit g^*. We clearly have that a social insurance for LTC is desirable with the ex post egalitarianism objective.

The paper of Leroux et al. (2021) revisits the design of optimal LTC insurance in comparing the utilitarian social criterion with two egalitarian social criteria—ex ante and ex post egalitarianism—which give priority to the worst-off either in expected or in realized terms. They show that the optimal second-best insurance under the ex-ante egalitarian criterion involves, in comparison to utilitarianism, higher LTC and pension benefits and higher tax rates on savings and on labor earnings. In comparison to ex ante egalitarianism, ex post egalitarianism involves lower LTC and pension benefits, a higher tax on savings, and a lower tax rate on labor earnings, in order to increase consumption of the young, who include persons who will turn out to be short-lived. In their analysis, living a longer life with disability is preferred to dying prematurely.

We can now summarize this section as follows. When individuals differ only in their risk of dependency, the ex-post egalitarian criterion favors dependent individuals more than the utilitarian criterion. When differences involve both the risk of dependency and the probability of premature death, this result holds if premature death is perceived as a preferable outcome to dependency. However, if this is not the case, the egalitarian criterion prioritizes individuals facing premature death but does not grant dependent individuals more favorable treatment than the utilitarian criterion would.

If disabled elderly individuals have lower marginal utility than their healthy counterparts, this provides a compelling explanation for the underdeveloped long-term care (LTC) insurance market. Under this scenario, even a utilitarian government might reasonably conclude that providing such insurance is unnecessary. However, if the government prioritizes ex post utility equalization, a strong case emerges for social insurance coverage of LTC.

4.2 Social Insurance with Family Assistance

4.2.1 Basic Model

As discussed in the subsection on the long-term care insurance puzzle, one key reason for the near absence of private insurance in most countries is the expectation that children will provide assistance in case of disability in old age. However, as we will now explore, private insurance does not operate in isolation—it can influence the level of informal care provided by children and shape public policy, particularly when it is actuarially fair. The basic model used involves parent-child families, where children's contributions to their elderly parents' care depend on their individual market productivity and their degree of altruism. Families differ in the levels of wages w_i and ω_i of the parent and the child and the disability risk π_i. Parent's lifetime utility can be written as:

$$U_i^p = u(w_i(1-\tau)l_i - s_i - I_i - v(l_i)) + (1-\pi_i)\,u(s_i) + \pi_i H\,(a_i, I_i/\pi_i + s_i + g)$$

where $H(a, m)$ is the LTC utility that depends on informal care provided by children, a_i, and formal cares $m_i = I_i/\pi_i + s_i + g$, financed by the actuarially fair insurance scheme I_i, saving s_i and public LTC benefit, g. LTC public benefits are financed by a payroll tax paid by the parents when young. A word on the LTC utility function $H(a, m)$ is in order. In the theoretical literature, this utility has most often just an argument, which means that formal and informal care are perfect substitutes. Another specification consists in distinguishing between standard consumption c and health status h, in which case we have $H(c, h)$. This specification is often used in health economics. In this section, we deliberately distinguish between formal and informal care and focus on whether these two types of care are substitutes or complements. To simplify the presentation, we assume zero interest rate and no time preference.

The timing of the game is the following:

1. The government chooses the tax rate and the benefit level that maximize the parents' welfare.
2. Parents choose their labor supply, their savings, and the LTC insurance premium, if any.
3. Children help their parents in case of disability.

Child's problem As standard, we proceed backward and thus look first at the child problem. The child's utility depends on whether the parent is dependent or not. It can be written as:

- in case of healthy parent: $U_i^c = u(d_i) = u(\omega_i)$
- in case of disabled parent: $U_i^c = u(d_i) + \beta H(a_i, m_i) = u(\omega_i(1 - a_i)) + \beta H(a_i, m_i)$,

where β denotes the degree of altruism and $m_i = I_i/\pi_i + s_i + g$ denotes formal care.

When the parent is healthy, the child consumes his/her earning ω_i. In case of loss of autonomy, he/she devotes a fraction of time a_i to caring. The FOC that defines the optimal a_i is simply

$$\Delta = -u'(d_i)\omega_i + \beta H_1(a_i, m_i) = 0.$$

From this condition, we obtain a supply function for caring time: $a_i = a(m_i; \beta, \omega_i)$. Differentiating the above FOC, we get:

$$\frac{\partial a_i}{\partial m_i} = \frac{\beta H_{12}}{-\Delta_{a_i}} \lesseqgtr 0 \Leftrightarrow H_{12} \lesseqgtr 0.$$

Note that in the separable case where $H_{12} = 0$, elder care would only depend on ω_i and β. In case of complementarity, elder care increases with m_i and in case of substitutability, we have some crowding out. We might be interested by the effect of ω_i on a_i. This can be obtained by differentiating the above FOC:

$$\frac{da_i}{d\omega_i} = \frac{u'(d_i)[R_R(d_i) - 1]}{-\Delta_{a_i}}$$

In other words, the effect of ω_i on a_i is positive or negative depending on whether the coefficient of relative risk aversion is higher or lower than 1. Here, we posit that the relative risk aversion coefficient as well as the distribution of children's wages are such that they have a small impact on informal care.

Throughout this analysis, we assume that children care only for their disabled parents out of altruism, meaning they do not provide assistance when their parents are healthy. Additionally, we intentionally selected altruism as the primary motive for caregiving. An alternative explanation could be the influence of social norms, in which case informal care would remain independent of the variable m_i.[7]

Parent's problem Before knowing his/her health status, the parent chooses l_i, s_i and I_i so as to maximize lifetime expected utility U_i^P subject to the caring function $a\left(m_i; \beta, \omega_i\right)$.

Parent's lifetime utility can be written as:

$$U_i^P = u(w_i(1-\tau)l_i - s_i - I_i - v(l_i)) + (1-\pi_i)\, u(s_i) + \pi_i H\left(a_i, I_i/\pi_i + s_i + g\right)$$

The FOCs are:

$$w_i(1-\tau) - v'(l_i) = 0$$

$$-\,u'(c_i) + (1-\pi_i)\, u'(s_i) + \pi_i H_2\left(a_i, m_i\right) + \pi_i H_1\left(a_i, m_i\right) \frac{\partial a_i}{\partial s_i} = 0$$

$$-\,u'(c_i) + H_2\left(a_i, m_i\right) + \pi_i H_1\left(a_i, m_i\right) \frac{\partial a_i}{\partial I_i} \leq 0.$$

where $\frac{\partial a_i}{\partial I_i} = \frac{\partial a_i}{\partial m_i}\frac{1}{\pi_i}$ and $\frac{\partial a_i}{\partial s_i} = \frac{\partial a_i}{\partial I_i} = \frac{\partial a_i}{\partial g} = \frac{\partial a_i}{\partial m_i}$. Note that granted that the Inada conditions apply to $u(d)$, the FOC with respect to s is always interior.

In case of interior solution with $I_i > 0$,we have:

$$-\,u'(c_i) + H_2\left(a_i, m_i\right) + \pi_i H_1\left(a_i, m_i\right) \frac{\partial a_i}{\partial I_i} = 0;\; u'(c_i) = u'(s_i).$$

Otherwise, when $I_i = 0$, we have

$$-\,u'(c_i) + H_2\left(a_i, m_i\right) + \pi_i H_1\left(a_i, m_i\right) \frac{\partial a_i}{\partial I_i} < 0.$$

We will consider those two cases.

Government's problem

Interior Solution

We now turn to the social welfare maximization when $I_i > 0$. We posit that the government is only concerned by the welfare of the elderly generation. We write the following Lagrangian to be maximized:

$$\mathcal{L} = E\{u(w(1-\tau)l - s - I - v(l)) + (1-\pi)\, u(s) + \pi H\left(a\left(.\right), I/\pi + s + g\right)$$
$$+\,\mu\left[\tau w l - \pi g\right]\},$$

[7] Klimaviciute et al. (2017).

where $Ez = \sum n_i z_i$ and μ denotes the multiplier associated with the revenue constraint.

We obtain the FOCs:

$$\frac{\partial \mathcal{L}}{\partial g} = E\left[\left(-u'(c) + (1-\pi)\, u'(d) + \pi H_2\right)\frac{\partial s}{\partial g} + \left(-u'(c_i) + H_2\right)\frac{\partial I}{\partial g} + \pi H_2. \right.$$
$$\left. + \pi H_1 \frac{da}{dg} - \mu\pi \right] = 0$$

$$\frac{\partial \mathcal{L}}{\partial \tau} = -E\left[u'(c)wl - \mu\left(wl + \tau w\frac{\partial l}{\partial \tau}\right)\right] = 0.$$

Using the FOCs of the parent:

$$\frac{\partial \mathcal{L}}{\partial g} = E\left[-\pi H_1[\frac{\partial a}{\partial s}\frac{\partial s}{\partial g} + \frac{\partial a}{\partial I}\frac{\partial I}{\partial g}] + \pi H_2 + \pi H_1\frac{da}{dg} - \mu\pi\right] = 0$$

or

$$\frac{\partial \mathcal{L}}{\partial g} = E\left[\pi H_2 + \pi H_1\frac{\partial a}{\partial g} - \mu\pi\right] = 0$$

where we have used the equality: $\frac{da_i}{dg} = \frac{\partial a_i}{\partial m_i}\left[1 + \frac{\partial m_i}{\partial s_i}\frac{\partial s_i}{\partial g} + \frac{\partial m_i}{\partial I_i}\frac{\partial I_i}{\partial g}\frac{1}{\pi}\right].$

Combining those two FOCs, we obtain the compensated effect of the tax denoted $\frac{\partial \mathcal{L}^C}{\partial \tau} = \frac{\partial \mathcal{L}^C}{\partial \tau} + \frac{dg}{d\tau}\frac{\partial \mathcal{L}}{\partial g}$:

$$\frac{\partial \mathcal{L}^C}{\partial \tau} = -Eu'(c)wl + E\pi H_2\frac{Ewl}{E\pi} + E\pi H_1\frac{\partial a}{\partial m}\frac{Ewl}{E\pi} + \mu\tau Ew\frac{\partial l}{\partial \tau} = 0$$

This can be rewritten as:

$$\frac{\partial \mathcal{L}^C}{\partial \tau} = -Eu'(c)wl + E\pi H_2\frac{Ewl}{E\pi} + E\pi\left(u'(c_i) - H_2\right)\frac{Ewl}{E\pi} + \mu\tau Ew\frac{\partial l}{\partial \tau} = 0,$$

or

$$\frac{\partial \mathcal{L}^C}{\partial \tau} = -cov\left(u'(c), wl\right) + cov\left(u'(c), \pi\right)\frac{Ewl}{E\pi} + \mu\tau Ew\frac{\partial l}{\partial \tau} = 0.$$

And thus:

$$\tau = \frac{-cov\left(u'(c), wl\right) + cov\left(u'(c), \pi\right)\frac{Ewl}{E\pi}}{-\mu Ew\frac{\partial l}{\partial \tau}}$$

The first covariance is clearly negative. Given that it is generally assumed that the risk of disability is negatively correlated with income, the second covariance is positive. We thus have that in case of interior solutions, family solidarity does not affect public LTC insurance. In this case, private insurance neutralizes the insurance role of the public scheme.

LTC Insurance Unavailable

Let us now assume that for the various reasons that are discussed within the issue of the LTC insurance puzzle (see Pestieau and Ponthiére (2012)),[8] such insurance does not exist. The choice of the parent is thus reduced to l_i and s_i that are used to maximize lifetime expected utility U_i^p subject to the caring function $a\,(m_i;\,\beta,\omega_i)$.

The problem of the government is expressed by the following Lagrangian to be maximized:

$$\mathcal{L} = E\{u(w(1-\tau)l - s - v(l)) + (1-\pi)\,u(s) + \pi H\,(a\,(.)\,, s+g) \\ + \mu\,[\tau wl - \pi g]\}.$$

Interior solutions are obvious here and thus, we obtain the FOCs:

$$\frac{\partial \mathcal{L}}{\partial g} = E\left[\pi H_1 \frac{\partial a}{\partial m} + \pi H_2 - \mu\pi\right] = 0$$

$$\frac{\partial \mathcal{L}}{\partial \tau} = -E\left[u'(c)wl - \mu\left(wl + \tau w\frac{\partial l}{\partial \tau}\right)\right] = 0.$$

Combining those two FOCs, we obtain the compensated effect of the tax

$$\frac{\partial \mathcal{L}^C}{\partial \tau} = -E\left[u'(c)wl - \pi H_2 \frac{Ewl}{E\pi} - \pi H_1 \frac{\partial a}{\partial m}\frac{Ewl}{E\pi} - \mu\tau w\frac{\partial l}{\partial \tau}\right] =$$

$$-\,cov\left(u'(c), wl\right) + cov\left(\pi, H_2\right)\frac{Ewl}{E\pi} + EwlE\left[H_2 - u'(c)\right] + \\ E\pi H_1 \frac{\partial a}{\partial m}\frac{Ewl}{E\pi} - \mu\tau Ew\frac{\partial l}{\partial \tau} = 0.$$

And thus:

$$\tau = \frac{-cov\left(u'(c), wl\right) + cov\left(\pi, H_2\right)\frac{Ewl}{E\pi} + EwlE\left[H_2 - u'(c)\right] + E\pi H_1 \frac{\partial a}{\partial m}\frac{Ewl}{E\pi}}{-\mu Ew\frac{\partial l}{\partial \tau}}$$

The first covariance is clearly negative, and the second is positive. The third term is expected to be positive. Indeed, in the First Best, we have that $H_2 - u'(c) = 0$,

[8] This subsection relies extensively on Nishimura & Pestieau 2025).

which can be implemented with an actuarial fair private insurance. In the absence of such insurance, the level of m is suboptimal. As to the last term of the denominator, it is positive as long as $H_{12} > 0$. We thus have that family solidarity fosters public spending in case of complementarity between a and m. In case of substitutability, it depresses public spending.

4.2.2 *Heterogeneity in Altruism and Productivity*

Jousten et al. (2005) examine a scenario involving families each made up of one young person and one elderly dependent who lacks financial resources. They assume all young individuals earning the same income while their levels of altruism vary. The government does not observe the level of altruism. The study investigates the effects of public long-term care interventions, including services like public nursing home care combined with a lump-sum subsidy for children who finance home care for their parents. The paper highlights how the government's inability to assess the level of children's altruism necessitates maintaining a relatively low quality of public nursing homes so as to avoid that altruistic children use the public facility for their disabled parents. Additionally, the study assesses the welfare outcomes for different groups within this framework.

In the above paper, children's wages were uniform and altruism differed across children. Assuming instead uniform altruism and variable wages, Pestieau and Sato (2008) explore a model involving parent-child families, where children's contributions to their elderly parents' care depend on their individual market productivity. In a laissez-faire environment, altruistic children with lower productivity tend to provide physical caregiving, while those with higher productivity provide financial support. Introducing private LTC insurance changes the dynamics, as children with intermediate productivity levels might opt for purchasing rather than providing direct support. The study delves into optimal public policies, which include a linear tax on children's earnings, a uniform subsidy for caregiving children, public nursing home options, and subsidies for private insurance premiums. The paper finds that using a combination of these tools, such as a high tax and subsidy rate, is particularly effective in scenarios where children generally have lower productivity and parents possess limited resources. It also highlights a robust case for public nursing services, particularly when private LTC insurance is not sufficiently efficient.

4.2.3 *Random Altruism*

When disabled parents rely on family members for care and assistance, various life events can disrupt these support systems without warning. Let us cite the most notable of these disruptions. Death of caregivers creates an immediate and often permanent gap in support. When an adult child who provides daily assistance passes away, the disabled parent may be left without their primary caregiver and emotional support. Illness can affect caregivers limiting their ability to provide care. Migration for employment, education, or personal reasons can physically separate caregivers from those who need care. Economic hardship can reduce the caregiver's availability. Finally, family disputes and relationship breakdowns can sever caregiving arrangements.

These disruptions modify the design of public policy as we now see. The child's problem is unchanged. We thus turn to the parent's problem.

Parent's problem Let us denote the uniform probability of informal care by ζ. This means that with a probability $1-\zeta$, the disabled parent does not receive any informal care ($a=0$).

The lifetime utility of the parent facing a probability π of becoming disabled and a probability of getting aid from the child ζ is the following

$$U_i^p = u(w_i(1-\tau)l_i - s_i - I_i - v(l_i)) + (1-\pi)\,u(s_i)$$

$$+\,\pi_i\,(1-\zeta)\,H\,(0, I_i/\pi_i + s_i + g) + \pi_i\zeta\,H\,(a_i, I_i/\pi_i + s_i + g)$$

The FOCs are:

$$w_i(1-\tau) - v'(l_i) = 0$$

$$-\,u'(c_i) + (1-\pi_i)\,u'(s_i) + \pi_i\zeta\left[H_2\,(a_i, m_i) + H_1\,(a_i, m_i)\,\frac{\partial a_i}{\partial m_i}\right]$$

$$+\,\pi_i\,(1-\zeta)\,H_2\,(0, m_i) = 0$$

$$-\,u'(c_i) + \zeta\left[H_2\,(a_i, m_i) + H_1\,(a_i, m_i)\,\frac{\partial a_i}{\partial m_i}\right] + (1-\zeta)\,[H_2\,(0, m_i)] \leq 0.$$

Government's problem The problem of the government is to maximize the following Lagrangian:

$$\mathcal{L} = E\{u(w(1-\tau)l - s - I - v(l)) + (1-\pi)\,u(s) + \pi\,(1-\zeta)\,H\,(0, m)$$

$$+\,\pi\zeta\,H\,(a, m) + \mu\,[\tau wl - \pi g]\}$$

Using the FOCs of the parent, we get the following FOCs:

$$\frac{\partial \mathcal{L}}{\partial g} = E\left[\zeta\pi\,H_1(a, m)\frac{\partial a}{\partial g} + \pi\,\Xi\,H_2 - \mu\pi\right] = 0,$$

$$\frac{\partial \mathcal{L}}{\partial \tau} = -E\left[u'(c)wl - \mu\left(wl + \tau w \frac{\partial l}{\partial \tau}\right)\right] = 0,$$

where $\varXi H_2 = \zeta H_2(a, m) + (1 - \zeta) H_2(0, m)$ is the expected marginal utility of formal care.

We now combine those two equations to obtain:

$$\frac{\partial \mathcal{L}^C}{\partial \tau} = -E\left[u'(c)wl - \pi \varXi H_2 \frac{Ewl}{E\pi} - \pi\zeta H_1(a, m) \frac{\partial a}{\partial m}\frac{Ewl}{E\pi} - \mu\tau w \frac{\partial l}{\partial \tau}\right]$$

$$= -cov\left(u'(c), wl\right) + \varXi cov(\pi, H_2)\frac{Ewl}{E\pi}$$

$$- Ewl\left[Eu'(c) - \varXi H_2\right] + \zeta E\pi H_1(a, m)\frac{\partial a}{\partial m}\frac{Ewl}{E\pi} - \mu\tau Ew\frac{\partial l}{\partial \tau} = 0,$$

where $\varXi cov(\pi, H_2) = \zeta cov(\pi, H_2(a, m)) + (1 - \zeta) cov(\pi, H_2(0, m))$ is the expected value of the covariance between the disability risk and the marginal utility of formal care.

We distinguish two cases. If $I > 0$, from the FOC of the parent, we can rewrite this equation as:

$$\frac{\partial \mathcal{L}^C}{\partial \tau} = -cov\left(u'(c), wl\right) + cov\left(u'(c), \pi\right)\frac{Ewl}{E\pi} + \mu\tau Ew\frac{\partial l}{\partial \tau} = 0$$

.

And thus:

$$\tau = \frac{-cov\left(u'(c), wl\right) + cov\left(u'(c), \pi\right)\frac{Ewl}{E\pi}}{-\mu Ew\frac{\partial l}{\partial \tau}}$$

If instead, $I = 0$, we have

$$\tau = \frac{-cov\left(u'(c), wl\right) + \varXi cov(\pi, H_2)\frac{Ewl}{E\pi} + Ewl\left[Eu'(c) - \varXi H_2\right] + \zeta E\pi H_1(a, m)\frac{\partial a}{\partial m}\frac{Ewl}{E\pi}}{-\mu Ew\frac{\partial l}{\partial \tau}}.$$

To see the impact of ζ on the level taxation $[\tau(\zeta)]$,we look at the two extreme cases:

$$\tau(0) = \frac{-cov\left(u'(c), wl\right) + cov(\pi, H_2(0, m))\frac{Ewl}{E\pi}}{-\mu Ew\frac{\partial l}{\partial \tau}}$$

$$\tau(1) = \frac{-cov\left(u'(c), wl\right) + cov(\pi, H_2(a, m))\frac{Ewl}{E\pi} + E\pi H_1(a, m)\frac{\partial a}{\partial m}\frac{Ewl}{E\pi}}{-\mu Ew\frac{\partial l}{\partial \tau}}.$$

It appears that when $H_{12} = 0$, the two formulas, $\tau(0)$ and $\tau(1)$, are very similar. When $H_{12} > 0$, the level of public spending seems to benefit from an increase in ζ, whereas when $H_{12} < 0$, we observe the opposite effect. This is pretty intuitive. In case of separability, there is no interaction between g and a. Family solidarity thus has a negligible impact on the desired level of public spending. In case of strong complementarity between g and a, there is a clear link between formal and informal care. An increase in a makes public spending more attractive. Finally, in case of strong substitutability between a and g, an increase in family solidarity crowds out formal care and thus discourages public spending.

The risk of default of informal care has no impact on the level of social LTC spending when every individual purchases private insurance. In case private insurance is not available, the incidence depends on the sign of $H_{12.}$ In case of complementarity, family solidarity fosters public spending. In case of substitutability, it discourages it.

In the model discussed above, public benefits can be supplemented by insurance compensations and private savings but remain distinct from informal care. Much of the theoretical research on uncertainty in informal care assumes that informal and formal care are perfect substitutes while recognizing that public LTC programs generally follow one of the following two models of policy. The opting-out (OO) policy provides public LTC benefits but prohibits individuals from supplementing them with personal funds, meaning those who seek higher-quality care must forgo public support entirely. In contrast, the topping-up (TU) policy allows individuals to enhance public LTC benefits with private resources. Several notable contributions have shaped this field, including studies by Cremer et al. (2013, 2017), Canta et al. (2020) and Canta and Cremer (2021). Cremer et al. (2013) introduce a model in which the likelihood of children providing care is endogenous, shaped by the time and effort parents invest in child-rearing. Subsequent papers take a different approach, assuming this probability to be exogenous. In these later works, children's altruism is initially treated as a binary trait but is later refined by Canta et al. (2020) into a continuous spectrum of altruistic behaviors. Most of the literature focuses on individuals with identical characteristics, though Cremer et al. (2013) also consider heterogeneity among agents.

Cremer et al. (2013) analyze an OO model in which public LTC benefits entirely exclude the possibility of self-insurance or familial assistance. Building on this, Cremer et al. (2017) examine a TU scheme, allowing for supplementary care from family or the market alongside public benefits. Canta et al. (2020) introduce an opting-out-cum-transfers (OC) model, where individuals can choose between standalone public care or a combination of monetary transfers and private care. Further advancing this discussion, Canta and Cremer (2021) explore non-linear policies that adjust public LTC benefits based on observable levels of informal care, suggesting that more flexible policies may be more effective. The effectiveness of these policies varies under different conditions.

Cremer et al. (2017) and Canta et al. (2020) argue that the TU scheme generally cannot outperform private insurance unless the private market is actuarially unfair. Conversely, the OO and OC models may be more effective under certain conditions by protecting individuals against the absence of informal care. However, there is no definitive ranking between the TU and OO models; each has its advantages depending on the context. Canta and Cremer (2021) conclude that the optimal policy should be non-linear, increasing LTC benefits in proportion to the level of informal care rather than applying rigid, binary distinctions. These insights highlight the complexity of LTC policy design in the presence of uncertain altruism, emphasizing the importance of adaptable solutions that account for varying levels of family support.

More recently, Cremer & Gahvari extend this analysis within an overlapping-generations framework, considering steady-state equilibria under both full and asymmetric information. In their model, children's altruism is shaped by the time and attention they received in childhood. One of their key findings is that when public LTC assistance carries no stigma, OO policies tend to be more cost-effective than TU policies in both first- and second-best settings. Their work reinforces the idea that policy effectiveness depends on broader social and behavioral factors, further complicating the debate on optimal LTC provision.

4.3 Social LTC Policy and Bequests

Bequests and dependence in old age are closely intertwined for several reasons. In societies lacking public or private long-term care insurance, children of parents who endure prolonged disability receive smaller inheritances compared to those whose parents remain healthy until the end of their lives. This disparity suggests that funding LTC insurance through an inheritance tax could be beneficial. Moreover, the low subscription rate to private LTC insurance is often cited as evidence against altruistic bequest motives. The argument is that not purchasing insurance exposes potential bequests to significant risk, indicating a lack of concern for future heirs. However, research by Lockwood (2018) challenges this notion. He demonstrates that bequest motives actually lead to increased savings and reduced purchases of LTC insurance. According to Lockwood, bequests are intentional, whether they result from a healthy life or an early death, which influences financial behavior accordingly.

To illustrate the link between public LTC and inheritance taxation, we present a simple model. We consider individuals who live for two periods. They only differ by their productivity w_i. Consumption in period 1 is denoted by c_i, consumption in period 2 if healthy is denoted d_i and LTC in case of disability is denoted m_i . They work 1 unit of time in period 1. Moreover, at the end of period 2, they may leave bequests motivated by joy of giving. Bequests in case of good health are denoted b_i. In case of disability, they cannot afford to leave any bequest. Their preferences can be described by the lifetime expected utility:

$$U_i = u(c_i) + [\pi H(m_i) + (1 - \pi)(u(d_i) + v(b_i))]$$

where π is the probability of dependence. Let s_i denote saving in period 1, θ the tax rate on bequests and g the public LTC benefit. We can rewrite the lifetime utility of type i individuals as:

$$U_i = u(w_i - s_i) + [\pi\, (H(s_i + g) + (1-\pi)\,(u(s_i - b_i\,(1+\theta)) + v(b_i))]$$

where the rate of interest as well as the time preference are nil. The utility functions $u(.)$, $v(.)$, $H(.)$ are strictly concave. As usual, we assume that $H'(z) > u'(z)$ and $H(z) < u(z)$.

The FOCs from the individual i's utility maximization are:

$$u'(c_i) = \pi H'(m_i) + (1-\pi)\, u'(d_i);\; u'(d_i)\,(1+\theta) = v'\,(b_i)\,.$$

From these conditions, one obtains demand or supply functions for $s_i$and b_i with θ and g as arguments.

The revenue constraint is simply:

$$\sum n_i\,[\pi g - \theta\,(1-\pi)\,b_i] = 0.$$

The Lagrangian expression to be maximized with respect to g and θ is the following:

$$\mathcal{L} = \sum n_i\,\{U_i - \mu\,[\pi g - \theta\,(1-\pi)\,b_i]\}\,,$$

where μ is the multiplier associated with the revenue constraint.

Using the envelop theorem and the operator E, the FOCs are simply:

$$\frac{\partial \mathcal{L}}{\partial \theta} = -E\left\{(1-\pi)\,u'(d)b - \mu\,((1-\pi)\,b + \Delta_\theta)\right\}$$

$$\frac{\partial \mathcal{L}}{\partial g} = E\left\{\pi H'(m) - \mu\left(\pi + \Delta_g\right)\right\}$$

where $\Delta_z = \theta E\left[\pi\,(1-\pi)\,\frac{\partial b}{\partial z}\right]$ for $z = g, \theta$ denotes the indirect effect of policy tools on government revenue.

Assuming that $\theta = g = 0$, we write these conditions in compensated form:

$$\frac{\partial \mathcal{L}^C}{\partial \theta}_{|\theta=g=0} = -\,(1-\pi)\,E\left\{u'(d)b - H'(m)Eb\right\} = -\,(1-\pi)\left\{cov\left(u'(d), b\right) - E\left(H'(m) - u'(d)\right)Eb\right\} \tag{4.15}$$

Given that $H'(m) - u'(d) > 0$, one has that $\frac{\partial \mathcal{L}^C}{\partial \theta}_{|\theta=g=0} > 0$. In other words, taxing bequests to finance public LTC is desirable.

Note that, if we reformulate the problem by introducing different disability risk π_i, we would rewrite (4.15) as:

$$\frac{\partial \mathcal{L}^{\mathcal{C}}}{\partial \theta}_{|\theta=g=0} = -cov\left(u'(d), (1-\pi)\,b\right) + \frac{E\left((1-\pi)\,b\right)}{E\pi}\left[cov\left(H'(m), \pi\right) + E\pi\, E\left(H'(m) - u'(d)\right)\right] \tag{4.16}$$

Given the observed negative correlation between w and π, $cov\left(H'(m), \pi\right) > 0$, which reinforce the desirability of this way of financing public LTC.

The above model follows from Brunner (2012). Brunner explores the potential role of bequest taxes as a form of LTC insurance. In his analysis, a typical individual aims to leave an inheritance, lacks private LTC insurance or is underinsured, and cannot adjust his/her labor supply or consumption after becoming dependent. Brunner demonstrates that when LTC costs diminish an individual's ability to leave a bequest, a proportional bequest tax can mitigate this loss by adjusting the tax burden according to the size of the bequest. This mechanism introduces a lower efficiency loss compared to income or consumption taxes, leading to a discussion on optimizing tax and transfer systems for LTC.

Cremer et al. (2016) delve into a dynamic where both parents and children display altruistic behaviors, with children's altruism being potentially partial. When parents face the risk of dependency, they anticipate support from their children, who are influenced by both altruism and the prospect of an inheritance. Their paper argues that laissez-faire outcomes are inefficient if children are not completely altruistic and suggests that efficiency can be restored through policies such as linear subsidies for informal care, linear bequest taxes, and specific lump-sum transfers. In a more constrained policy environment without state-specific transfers, the study proposes that linear taxes on bequests and children's labor income can still provide partial insurance, echoing some of Brunner's (2012) findings.

Canta and Cremer (2019) examine a model inspired by the strategic bequest approach, where parents condition their bequests on the amount of informal care they receive. All parents are assumed to be identical, while children differ in their care provision costs, a proxy for factors like altruism or opportunity costs. Due to asymmetric information where parents cannot see these costs, they cannot fully harness the potential exchange benefits, leading to suboptimal care levels from higher-cost children under laissez-faire conditions. The paper considers two types of social LTC policies: a uniform policy that offers equal LTC transfers funded by a uniform tax, and more tailored policies that link LTC benefits to observable transfers between parents and children. While the first type does not completely shield parents from the risk of having a high-cost caregiver child, the second type provides comprehensive insurance against such risks. The study underscores that even with potential private insurance solutions, public intervention might still be justified due to different objectives between parents and the government, compounded by high costs and challenges associated with private insurance offerings. The above models rest on a government that maximizes a utilitarian social welfare function.

Leroux and Pestieau (2022) explore the optimal structure of taxes on bequests under both utilitarian and Rawlsian frameworks. Given the government's inability to ascertain whether bequests are intentional or accidental—but with access to data on timing and health status at death—they analyze how early bequests, late bequests when healthy and late bequests when disabled should be taxed. In the utilitarian approach, bequest taxes are influenced by equity, insurance, and public revenue considerations. Should equity concerns prevail, higher taxes are justified for those who live longer and in better health, whereas lower taxes apply to those who die sooner. Conversely, if insurance factors dominate, higher taxes would target early bequests, with reduced taxes on bequests under dependency conditions. Under Rawlsian principles, the optimal policy advocates minimal taxes on early bequests, while imposing higher taxes on bequests left by healthy, long-lived individuals.

4.4 The Rule of Reimbursement

We now move to the design of an insurance contract and the issue of whether we should opt for a contract based on coinsurance or on deductible. We keep in mind Arrow's underrated deductible theorem. This theorem states that, if an insurance company is willing to offer any insurance policy against loss desired by the buyer at a premium which depends only on the policy's actuarial value, then the policy chosen by a risk-averse buyer will take the form of 100% coverage above a deductible minimum.[9] This theorem rests on the existence of loading costs. Otherwise, there would be a 100% insurance coverage. It implies that an insurance with deductible dominates the more traditional policy based on coinsurance rates.

Following Drèze and Schokkaert (2013), Drèze et al. (2016) consider a simple example with S states of nature. A_s is the initial health status that decreases with s ($s = 1, 2, ..., S$). The final health status is denoted by $m_s = A_s + d_s$ where d_s represents the level of medical expenditures and at the same time the improvement in health. The individual has a given income w and a utility U_s that depends on consumption c_s and health m_s. The insurance rate is α_s, the insurance premium I and the loading factor λ. The rate of coinsurance is thus $1 - \alpha_s$. A direct application of this model is sickness or dependance. As s increases the severity of sickness grows or the number of months of dependence augments.

We first analyze the case where health spending is observable and then the case where it is not observable and can thus be influenced by the rate of reimbursement, which is the case with ex post moral hazard.[10]

4.4.1 No Moral Hazard

Individual utility is given by:

[9] Arrow (1963).

[10] In insurance economics, we distinguish between ex ante and ex post moral hazard. Ex ante moral hazard is a change in behavior prior to the outcome of the random event. Ex post moral hazard involves behavior after the outcome.

$$U_s = u(c_s) + h(m_s)$$

or

$$U_s = u(w - I - (1 - \alpha_s)\, d_s) + h(A_s + d_s)$$

The insurance premium is defined as:

$$I = (1 + \lambda) \sum_t^S \pi_t \alpha_t d_t.$$

We can now write the problem to be solved, namely, finding the values of d_s and α_s that maximize the following expected utility (denoted by $\mathcal{L}$):

$$\mathcal{L} = \sum_s^S \pi_s \left[u(w - (1 + \lambda) \sum_t^S \pi_t \alpha_t d_t - (1 - \alpha_s)\, d_s) + h(A_s + d_s) \right]$$

We obtain the FOCs:

$$\frac{\partial \mathcal{L}}{\partial d_s} = -u'(c_s)\,(1 - \alpha_s) + h'(m_s) - (1 + \lambda)\alpha_s \sum \pi_t u'(c_t) = 0$$

$$\frac{\partial \mathcal{L}}{\partial \alpha_s} = d_s \left[u'(c_s) - (1 + \lambda) \sum \pi_t u'(c_t) \right] \leq 0$$

This implies:

$$u'(c_s) = h'(m_s)$$

and we distinguish between two regimes of light and heavy disability according to the value of s with respect to a threshold value $\bar{s}$.

$$s < \bar{s} \Rightarrow \frac{\partial \mathcal{L}}{\partial \alpha_s} < 0 \Longrightarrow \alpha_s = 0$$

and

$$s > \bar{s} \Rightarrow \frac{\partial \mathcal{L}}{\partial \alpha_s} = 0 \Longrightarrow u'(c_s) = (1 + \lambda) \sum \pi_t u'(c_t) \Longrightarrow (1 - \alpha_s)\, d_s = F$$

In other words, for any expense below F there is no coverage. For any expense above F there is full coverage. F is the deductible.

Note that if $\lambda = 0$, $\alpha_s = 1$ and there is full coverage of any expense.

4.4.2 Moral Hazard

We know that introduces the possibility of ex post moral hazard. Now spending is not observable and chosen by the individual given the value of α. This amounts to:

$$Max_{d_s} = u(w - I - (1 - \alpha_s)\, d_s) + h(A_s + d_s).$$

The FOC is:

$$- u'(c_s)(1 - \alpha_s) + h'(m_s) = 0.$$

We thus have $d(\alpha_s)$ with $\frac{\partial d_s}{\partial \alpha_s} > 0$. The problem of the insurer is thus to find the values of α_s that maximize:

$$\mathcal{L} = \sum p_s \left[u(w - (1 + \lambda) \sum \pi_t \alpha_t d_t - (1 - \alpha_s)\, d_s) + h(A_s + d_s) \right]$$

The solution is not necessarily interior, and the FOC is written as:

$$\frac{\partial \mathcal{L}}{\partial \alpha_s} = \left[-u'(c_s)\,(1 - \alpha_s) + h'(m_s) - (1 + \lambda)\alpha_s \sum \pi_t u'(c_t) \right] \frac{\partial d_s}{\partial \alpha_s} +$$

$$d_s \left[u'(c_s) - (1 + \lambda) \sum \pi_t u'(c_t) \right] \leq 0.$$

or

$$\frac{\partial \mathcal{L}}{\partial \alpha_s} = d_s u'(c_s) - \left[(1 - \alpha_s)\, u'(c_s) \frac{\partial d_s}{\partial \alpha_s} - h'(m_s) \frac{\partial d_s}{\partial \alpha_s} \right] -$$

$$\left[d_s + \frac{\partial d_s}{\partial \alpha_s} \frac{\alpha_s}{d_s} \right] (1 + \lambda)(1 + \eta_s) \sum \pi_t u'(c_t) \leq 0$$

After simplifications, we obtain:

$$\frac{\partial \mathcal{L}}{\partial \alpha_s} = d_s \left[u'(c_s) - (1 + \lambda)(1 + \eta_s) \sum \pi_t u'(c_t) \right] \leq 0$$

where $\eta_s = \frac{\alpha_s \partial d_s}{d_s \partial \alpha_s} > 0$ is the elasticity of spending in state s with respect to the insurance rate. If $\eta_s = \bar{\eta}$ is constant, c_s is constant and the deductible is $(1 - \alpha_s)\, d_s = F$ with $\frac{dF}{d\bar{\eta}} > 0$. Whether this elasticity is constant is an empirical question.

4.4.3 Social Insurance with Deductible

Starting from the above model, Klimaviciute and Pestieau (2018a) analyze optimal social LTC insurance under conditions of varying productivity and LTC needs, focusing on contracts with deductibles. They find that optimal public policy should mirror private insurance practices using deductibles if the government and private insurers have similar operational costs. The necessity for public intervention grows if the government can operate more efficiently than private insurers or if there are significant variations in LTC needs across individuals. In Klimaviciute and Pestieau (2018b), the study extends to a more diverse society with differing income levels and dependency risks, assuming a strong inverse relationship between these factors. They explore more constrained public policies, suggesting that negative or zero deductibles could be optimal due to redistributive needs, despite potential increases in cost.[11] Even with private insurance options, their findings imply that not all individuals would choose to insure privately at the social optimum, pointing toward a blended approach of public and private insurance solutions under specific conditions.

4.5 Spending Down

We now present a simple model aimed at discussing two methods for discouraging middle-class individuals from utilizing a social assistance program for long-term care (LTC) that is intended for low-income individuals.[12] The first method involves raising the wealth threshold that individuals can possess at the onset of their disability. The second method is to implement a look-back period to assess whether individuals exceeded this threshold in the past. In this simple model, we focus on the old age that is divided in three periods. At the start, individuals are just characterized by their initial wealth w. They further earn an income z during the first two periods.

During the first two periods, individuals are healthy. In each period, individuals' utility depends on their consumption c_t with $t = 1, 2, 3$ and the transfers b_t they make to their children. At the start of the third period, they run the risk of becoming dependent with probability π. In case of disability, they can use part of their savings to finance their long-term care m or use means tested services denoted g. In case of disability, they make a transfer b_d to their children, whereas in case of good health they leave a bequest of b_3. In this model, we make two simplifying assumptions. First, topping up is not allowed meaning that g cannot be combined with private services. Second, we are not concerned by the way g is financed. LTC services are only available to disabled elderly if their wealth at the start of the third period is less than a certain amount x. There is thus a wealth level w for which individuals are indifferent between resorting to the public scheme and self-financing their long-term care. To limit access to the public LTC program, the government may decide that this wealth limit should be imposed at the start of the second period. As we shall see, the introduction of this look-back period has the effect of increasing first-period inter-vivos gifts (b_1) but reducing second-period ones (b_2).

[11] See also Klimaviciute and Pestieau (2020).

[12] Lozachmeur et al. (2025).

We consider three cases that will lead to partitioning our society along the variable w. We present the lifetime utility under these different regimes. It will be denoted U^j, where $j = A, B, C$.

- A. Not using Medicaid

$$U^A = u(c_1) + v(b_1) + \beta\,[u(c_2) + v(b_2)] + \beta^2$$
$$[\pi\,(H(m) + v(b_d)) + (1-\pi)\,(u(c_3) + v(b_3))]$$

or more explicitly

$$U^A = u(w + z - b_1 - s_1) + v(b_1) + \beta\,[u(s_1 R + z - b_2 - s_2) + v(b_2)]$$
$$+ \beta^2\,[\pi\,(H(s_2 R - b_d) + v(b_d)) + (1-\pi)\,(u(s_2 - b_3) + v(b_3))]$$

- B. No look back period. Resources ceiling: x

$$U^B = u(c_1) + v(b_1) + \beta\,[u(c_2) + v(b_2)]$$
$$+ \beta^2\,[\pi\,(H(g) + v(b_d)) + (1-\pi)\,(u(c_3) + v(b_3))]$$

or

$$U^B = u(w + z - b_1 - s_1) + v(b_1) + \beta\,[u(s_1 R + z - b_2 - x) + v(b_2)]$$
$$+ \beta^2\,[\pi\,(H(g) + v(xR)) + (1-\pi)\,(u(xR - b_3) + v(b_3))]$$

We assume that $x < s_2$, which means that the individual would have liked to save more than x, but chooses not to do so to enjoy g.

- C. One look back period. Resources ceiling: x

$$U^C = u(c_1) + v(b_1) + \beta\,[u(c_2) + v(b_2)]$$
$$+ \beta^2\,[\pi\,(H(g) + v(b_d)) + (1-\pi)\,(u(c_3) + v(b_3))]$$

or

$$U^C = u(w + z - b_1 - x) + v(b_1) + \beta\,[u(xR + z - b_2 - s_2) + v(b_2)]$$
$$+ \beta^2\,[\pi\,(H(g) + v(s_2 R)) + (1-\pi)\,(u(s_2 R - b_3) + v(b_3))]$$

We here assume that $x < s_1$.

In this expression, $u(.)$, $v(.)$, $H(.)$ are strictly concave utility functions, R is the interest factor; β, the time preference factor; z, the income earned in the first two periods. The population can be partitioned into two groups: those who benefit from Medicaid and those who self-insure. When the public LTC program does not include a look-back period provision (case B), we have the individuals who finance their own LTC spending and those who resort to public LTC. The threshold wealth that separates those two groups is denoted w_{AB}, that is the level of wealth for which $U^A = U^B$.

Similarly we have w_{AC}, which is the level for which individuals are indifferent between case A and case C.

By differentiating $U^A - U^B = 0$ with respect to x and w, we have that:

$$\frac{dw_{AB}}{dx} = -\frac{u'(d^B) - v'(x)}{u'(c_1^A) - u'(c_1^B)} > 0$$

where $u'(d^B) - v'(x) < 0$ comes from the fact that the constraint x is binding. This implies that as the allowed wealth ceiling decreases, the number of benefiters from Medicaid decreases.

We are interested in the impact of the introduction of a look-back period. It can easily be shown that for the same w and x, $U^B > U^C$, which implies that introducing a look-back period deters some individuals from applying to the public LTC program. This is quite intuitive. In case C, the individual is left with an amount of resources x to finance his consumption and transfers in the second and third period whereas, in case B, he can use the same amount to finance both consumption and bequests in just the third period.

In our model, spending down occurs through intergenerational transfers. In the case B, the individual devotes all the allowed saving x to bequests in case of dependence. Decreasing x means decreasing bequests. If we move to case C with look-back, first and second period saving decreases further: $s_1^C = x < s_1^B$. and $s_2^C < s_1^B = x$. Hence, we have that $b_1^C > b_1^B$, $b_3^C < b_3^B$ and $b_2^C < b_2^B$. This leads us to the following conclusions. First, when the threshold x decreases, the number of users of public LTC decreases, the level of early transfers increases and the level of bequests decreases. Second, when a look-back period is introduced while keeping the threshold x constant, the number of users of public LTC decreases. First period inter-vivos gifts increase but later gifts and bequests decrease.

4.6 Capital Accumulation with LTC

Until now, we have employed a static framework. In this section, we extend the analysis to a dynamic setting to explore the impact of old-age disability and long-term care policies on capital accumulation and welfare. For this purpose, we utilize the canonical two-period overlapping generations model established by Diamond (1965) and Samuelson (1958). The model assumes a closed economy with perfect competitive markets.

4.6.1 Basic Model

Time is discrete, and in each period t, the economy features three goods: capital, labor, and a physical good produced using capital and labor.

Each individual belongs to a generation t and lives for up to two periods, resulting in two overlapping generations at any point in time. The first period of life has a unitary length; the individual works with an inelastic supply of labor and earns a wage w_t. This wage is devoted to present consumption c_t and saving s_t. The second period is uncertain and depends on a survival probability ϕ. If the individual survives, he/she will not work and consume d_t that is financed by the return of saving $s_t R_{t+1}/\phi$, where R_{t+1}/ϕ is the return of an actuarially fair annuity. $R_{t+1} = 1 + r_{t+1}$ is the interest factor and r_{t+1} is the interest rate. The lifetime utility of an individual belonging to generation t can be written as:

$$U_t = u(c_t) + \beta\phi u(d_t)$$

or

$$U_t = u(w_t - s_t) + \beta\phi u(s_t R_{t+1}/\phi)$$

where u(.) is strictly concave and β is the time preference factor. Note that we use the generation index for consumption and labor supply and the time index for the factor prices.

The optimization problem of an individual is to allocate labor income over the lifetime in order to maximize her utility. The first-order condition with respect to s_t is:

$$-u'(c_t) + \beta\phi R_{t+1} u'(d_t) = 0,$$

which means that the marginal utility of first-period consumption is equal to the marginal utility of second-period consumption multiplied by a factor equal to $\beta\phi R$. Turning to the production side, we assume a representative firm producing at period t with a simple constant return to scale technology such that aggregate output depends on the capital stock and the labor force:

$$Y = F(K_t, L_t)$$

where L_t denotes the labor force that is here equal to N_t, the size of generation t. Population grows at the rate n such that:

$$N_t = N_{t-1}(1 + n).$$

As one period represents a working life, it is reasonable to assume that the stock of capital fully depreciates at the end of a period. The stock of capital at time $t+1$ is thus equal to saving at time t.

$$K_{t+1} = N_t s_t$$

The objective of the representative firm is to maximize profit and the condition for a maximum profit is:

$$R_t = F_K(K_t, L_t);\ w_t = F_L(K_t, L_t)$$

or, in intensive terms, with $k = K/N$ and $y = Y/N = f(k)$,

$$R_t = f'(k_t);\ w_t = f(k_t) - f'(k_t)k_t.$$

As it is standard in the literature, we use the logarithmic function for utility and the Cobb-Douglas function for the production, namely

$$U_t = log(w_t - s_t) + \beta\phi log(s_t R_{t+1}/\phi)$$

and

$$Y = AK^{\alpha}L^{1-\alpha},$$

where A is the total factor productivity (which is constant) and $0 < \alpha < 1$. With these functional forms, we have that:

$$(1+n)k_{t+1} = s_t = \frac{\phi\beta}{1+\phi\beta}w_t = \frac{\phi\beta}{1+\phi\beta}(1-\alpha)Ak_t^{\alpha}.$$

The inter-temporal equilibrium is characterized by the dynamics of the stock of capital k_t and the model converges to a steady state that is given by:

$$k^{SS} = \left[\frac{\phi\beta A}{1+\phi\beta}\frac{1-\alpha}{1+n}\right]^{\frac{1}{1-\alpha}}$$

with $\frac{\partial k^{SS}}{\partial \pi} > 0$; $\frac{\partial k^{SS}}{\partial n} < 0$. Hence, population aging because of an increase in ϕ (but also because of a fall in n) increases the per capita capital stock.

It is interesting to contrast the market solution obtained from the maximization of the utility of a single generation with the solution that would maximize total welfare in the steady state. This social optimum is obtained by maximizing the generational utility $U = u(c) + \phi\beta u(d)$ subject to the resource constraint:

$$f(k) = k(1+n) + c + \frac{\phi d}{1+n}.$$

We thus have to find the values of k and d that maximize the lifetime utility:

$$U = u\left[f(k) - k(1+n) - \frac{\phi d}{1+n}\right] + \phi\beta u\,(d)\,.$$

The first-order conditions are:

$$f'(k_t) = (1+n) \tag{4.17}$$

$$u'(c) = (1+n)\,\beta u'(d)$$

where (4.17) is the Golden rule level of capital accumulation. It is defined by the equality of the growth rate of the population n with the marginal productivity of capital. With the Cobb-Douglas production function, the optimal capital accumulation is $k^* = (\frac{\alpha A}{1+n})^{\frac{1}{1-\alpha}}$. It is generally admitted that $1+r = f'(k) > 1+n$. This condition means that the economy is dynamically efficient, namely in a state of under-accumulation. Note that unlike k^{SS}, k^* depends on n but not on either ϕ or β.

4.6.2 Disability in Old Age

We introduce the probability π of getting old and dependent along with the probability ϕ of surviving beyond the first period. We assume a fair annuity market as well as a fair LTC insurance market. We write the lifetime utility of an individual belonging to generation t as:

$$U_t = u(w_t - s_t - I_t) + \beta\left[\phi(1-\tau)u(s_t R_{t+1}/\phi) + \pi H(s_t R_{t+1}/\phi + I_t R_{t+1}/\phi\pi\right]$$

where I_t is the LTC insurance premium. With first look at the market solution when there is a LTC insurance and then we assume away such insurance, but introduce some LTC public policy.

Market solution with LTC insurance Maximizing U_t with respect to s_t and I_t yields the FOCs:

$$u'(c_t) = \beta R_{t+1}\left[(1-\pi)u'(d_t) + \pi H'(m_t)\right] \tag{4.18}$$

$$u'(c_t) = \beta R_{t+1} H'(m_t) \tag{4.19}$$

Combining (4.18) and (4.19) yields:

$$u'(c_i) = \beta R_{t+1} u'(d_t)$$

Turning to the log specification, we have

$$U_t = log(w_t - s_t - I_t) + \beta\phi\left[(1-\pi)log(s_t R_{t+1}/\phi)\right.$$
$$\left.+\pi\ (\kappa log(s_t R_{t+1}/\phi + I_t R_{t+1}/\pi\phi) - a)\right]$$

where the parameters $a > 0$ and $\kappa > 1$ give the desired property that $H'(z) > u'(z)$ and $H(z) < u(z)$. With this specification, the FOCs become:

$$\frac{1}{w_t - s_t - I_t} = \frac{\beta\kappa}{s_t/\phi + I_t/\pi\phi} = \frac{\beta\phi(1-\pi)}{s_t} + \frac{\pi\kappa\beta}{s_t/\phi + I_t/\pi\phi)} \tag{4.20}$$

From (4.20), we get:

$$I_t = s_t\pi(\kappa - 1) \tag{4.21}$$

Combining (4.20) and (4.21), we obtain the expression for capital accumulation: $(1+n)k_{t+1} = s_t + I_t = \frac{\phi\beta(1+\pi(\kappa-1))}{1+\phi\beta(1+\pi(\kappa-1))}(1-\alpha)k_t^{\alpha}$.

This can be rewritten as:

$$(1+n)k_{t+1} = S(1-\alpha)k_t^{\alpha}$$

where $S = \frac{\phi\beta(1+\pi(\kappa-1))}{1+\phi\beta(1+\pi(\kappa-1))}$ can be considered as the saving rate that is time invariant in this particular case. In the steady state, we get:

$$k^{SS} = \left[S\frac{1-\alpha}{1+n}\right]^{\frac{1}{1-\alpha}}$$

One observes that S as well as k^{SS} increase with both ϕ and π. In other words, both the survival probability and the disability risk foster capital accumulation. The first increases the need for retirement savings, and the second, the needs for LTC spending.

Market solution without LTC insurance but with a subsidy on LTC. We now assume that there is no LTC insurance, but that the government introduce a subsidy on LTC spending that is financed by a payroll tax τ. Keeping the log example, we now write the lifetime utility of a member of generation t as:

$$U_t = log(w_t(1-\tau_t) - s_t) + \beta\phi$$
$$\left[(1-\pi)log\left(s_t\frac{R_{t+1}}{\phi}\right) + \pi\left(\kappa log\left(\left(s_t\frac{R_{t+1}}{\phi}(1+\sigma)\right)\right) - a\right)\right]$$

where σ is the subsidy rate that is time invariant. Underlying this tax-subsidy scheme, we have the revenue constraint that:

$$\tau_t w_t = \sigma\pi s_{t-1}R_t/\phi$$

With this specification, the FOCs become:

$$\frac{1}{w_t(1-\tau_t)-s_t}=\frac{\beta\phi(1-\pi)}{s_t}+\frac{\pi\kappa\beta}{s_t} \tag{4.22}$$

and hence:

$$s_t = Sw_t(1-\tau_t) \tag{4.23}$$

From (4.23), we obtain the expression for capital accumulation: $(1+n)k_{t+1} = (1-\tau_t)(1-\alpha)Sk_t^{\alpha}$. In the steady state, we get:

$$k^{SS}=\left[S\frac{(1-\tau)(1-\alpha)}{1+n}\right]^{\frac{1}{1-\alpha}}$$

One easily check that k^{SS} increases with ϕ and π as above, but decreases with τ.

4.6.3 Social Optimum

We can now contrast these solutions with that obtained by looking at the social optimum. To do so, we have to find the values of c, d, k, m that maximize the lifetime utility in the steady-state

$$\begin{aligned}\mathcal{L} &= u(c)+\beta\phi\left[(1-\pi)u(d)+\pi H(m)\right]\\ &-\mu\left[c+\frac{\phi((1-\pi)d}{1+n}+\frac{\pi\phi m}{1+n}+(1+n)k-f(k)\right]\end{aligned}$$

We obtain the following FOCs:

$$f'(k)=1+n;\, u'(c)=\beta Ru'(d)=\beta RH'(m)=\mu.$$

The equality $f'(k)=1+n$ corresponds to the Golden rule and implies $k^*=\left[\frac{\alpha}{1+n}\right]^{\frac{1}{1-\alpha}}$ that is independent of either π and ϕ. The decentralization of this first-best optimum requires an intergenerational transfer scheme to achieve the golden rule and the presence of actuarially fair annuities and long-term care insurance.

To sum up, we have shown that if fair LTC insurance and annuity markets exist, we have in the steady state a level of capital and output that increases with the survival probability and the disability risk. In case there is no LTC insurance and the government subsidizes private LTC spending with a payroll tax, the tax implies a lower level of capital and output.

It is clear that lump sum transfers are generally not available, and one has to resort to distortionary instruments such as public pensions, long-term care public benefits, and income taxation. The problem is that there is a conflict between those instruments that tend to discourage saving and the achievement of dynamic efficiency. In a model with family assistance, Canta et al. (2016) reach an interesting result: public LTC insurance operates as a complement to private insurance and hence fosters capital accumulation. Ponthiere and Thibault (2025) also employ an overlapping generations model where survival probability depends on preventive health spending. They demonstrate that when considering the possibility of autonomy loss in old age, the joint improvement of economic and longevity outcomes—commonly referred to as the Preston Curve—is not observed.

4.7 Political Economy

While models focusing on the political economy of LTC are less prevalent than those dedicated to optimal policy design, they offer valuable insights into a variety of settings, from behavioral biases to family dynamics and the political feasibility of programs targeting the economically disadvantaged. These models generally find some level of political support for social LTC schemes, but this support can be undermined by factors such as familial obligations, behavioral misconceptions, competition with private insurance, or the inadequacy of proposed social programs. Ensuring broad-based political support, especially from the middle class, for social LTC programs aimed at the poor remains a complex and challenging endeavor. This complexity underscores the multifaceted nature of political sustainability in social LTC programs, akin to the intricacies of optimal policy design.

As an illustration of the problem at hand, we now present a simple model of vote over a social LTC scheme. In this model, LTC public benefit g is uniform and financed by a payroll tax τ. Family assistance is assumed away. Individuals differ only in their wage levels and disability risk. They can purchase actuarially fair LTC insurance. The lifetime utility of an individual with wage w_i can be written as follows:

$$U_i = u((1-\tau)\, w_i l_i - s_i - I_i - v(l_i)) + (1-\pi_i) u(s_i) + \pi_i H(s_i + g + I_i/\phi_i)$$

where $g = \tau \frac{\sum n_j w_j l_j}{\overline{\pi}}$ and $\overline{\pi} = \sum n_j \pi_j$

Maximizing U_i with respect to l_i, s_i, and I_i leads to the FOCs:

$$\frac{\partial U_i}{\partial l_i} = u'(c_i)\,[-w_i l_i\,(1-\tau) + v(l_i)] = 0$$

$$\frac{\partial U_i}{\partial s_i} = -u'(c_i) + \pi_i H'(m_i) + (1-\pi_i)\, u'(s_i) s_i = 0$$

$$\frac{\partial U_i}{\partial I_i} = -u'(c_i) + H'(m_i) \geq 0$$

Then we look at the tax rate that each individual of type i would choose. This is given by the FOC:

$$\frac{\partial U_i}{\partial \tau} = -u'(c_i)w_i l_i + \pi_i H'(m_i)\left[\frac{\overline{wl}}{\overline{\pi}} + \tau\frac{\sum n_j w_j \frac{\partial l_j}{\partial \tau}}{\overline{\pi}}\right] \geq 0$$

When the solution is interior, we can define the optimal value of the tax from the viewpoint of individuals of type i:

$$\tau^i = \frac{1 - \frac{w_i l_i}{\pi_i}\frac{\overline{\pi}}{\overline{wl}}}{-\frac{\sum n_j w_j \frac{\partial l_j}{\partial \tau}}{\overline{wl}}}$$

Differentiating U_i with respect to τ, it is straightforward to see that preferences over τ are concave (and thus single-peaked), so that we can apply the median voter theorem and obtain that there may exist a value of τ^* that is preferred by a majority of voters to any other value of τ. This majority-chosen level τ^* corresponds to the value of τ that is such that at least half the polity exhibits $\tau > \tau^*$ while at least half is such that $\tau < \tau^*$. In the case where $l_i = 1$, we observe that the set of agents who favor $\tau > 0$ is made of all agents with $\frac{w_i}{\pi_i} < \frac{\bar{w}}{\bar{\pi}}$.

Using such a model with family assistance, De Donder and Pestieau (2017) analyze how individual differences in income, risk of dependence, and family support affect preferences for social versus private insurance. Their results suggest that family support tends to decrease the demand for both types of insurance, especially private. Despite this, they find that most individuals would oppose a ban on private insurance, even though its presence reduces the chosen level of social insurance in voting scenarios.

Nuscheler and Roeder (2013) examine the impact of family dynamics on the support for public LTC. They model a society composed of single-parent families with varying child productivity. Their findings highlight a political conflict between families with and without disabled parents and between wealthy and less affluent families, illustrating how income inequality negatively correlates with public LTC spending. This relationship may shift with demographic changes influencing the demand for LTC and the corresponding supply of informal care.

De Donder and Leroux (2013) explore the dynamics of political support for social LTC insurance, accounting for behavioral biases in individual decision-making. Their model posits that all individuals face identical risks of dependency but have different perceptions and responses to these risks. They classify individuals into three groups based on their behavioral biases: sophisticated procrastinators, who underestimate their risk but correct this bias when voting; optimistic individuals, who underestimate only their personal risk while acknowledging the average risk; and myopic individuals, who underestimate both personal and average risks. The study finds that sophisticated procrastinators achieve optimal outcomes, whereas optimistic and myopic individuals tend to underinsure and over-save. Interestingly, in scenarios where private insurance is available, the more biased individuals fare worse off than in scenarios without private insurance options, except for the less biased optimists.

De Donder and Leroux (2017) explore a model where families consist of one elderly parent and one adult child. They find several reasons for the limited social LTC transfers, such as parents' preference for time over monetary help from their children and the potential opposition from disability free families to social LTC schemes.

Cremer et al. (2021) investigate the political viability of means-tested social programs, like Medicaid in the USA, in environments without familial aid. They propose a model where a Rawlsian government initially decides the likelihood of middle-class inclusion in these programs, followed by a majority vote on the level of benefits. Their findings indicate that the ideal probability of middle-class inclusion decreases with greater income inequality but increases with higher relative risk aversion among middle-class individuals.

Last Remark

This chapter, the most significant in this book, has explored the design of long-term care policies by presenting various models that address specific challenges. Given the complexity of the issues at stake, constructing a single, all-encompassing model is neither feasible nor realistic. However, a common thread runs through all the topics discussed: the imperative to consider both the family and the market when formulating optimal policies.

It is also worth noting that the literature on long-term care policy has grown substantially, making it impossible to provide an exhaustive overview. This chapter, therefore, offers a selective—and inevitably subjective—perspective on the key debates shaping the field.

Notation Used in This Chapter

- $U(.)$: lifetime utility
- $u(.)$: strictly concave utility function of consumption c or d
- $H(m)$: strictly concave utility function of LTC m
- $H(a, m)$: quasi concave utility of a, informal care, and m, formal care
- $h(l)$: strictly concave disutility of labor l
- $x = c - h(l)$: net consumption
- π : probability of disability
- ϕ : survival probability
- ζ : probability of informal care
- g : public LTC benefits
- w, ω : wage rates

- n_i : the relative number of type i's individuals
- P : public pension benefits
- $\mathcal{L}$: Lagrangian expression
- μ : Lagrange multiplier associated with the revenue constraint
- I : private insurance premium
- s : saving
- b : bequests
- θ, τ : tax rates
- λ : loading factor
- α_s : insurance rate

References

Arrow, K. (1963). Uncertainty and the welfare economics of medical care. *American Economic Review, 53*, 941–973.

Atkinson, A. B., & Stiglitz, J. E. (1976). The design of tax structure: Direct versus indirect taxation. *Journal of Public Economics, 6*, 55–75.

Brunner, J. (2012). *The bequest tax as long-term care insurance*. CESifo Discussion Paper.

Canta, C., & Cremer, H. (2019). Long-term care policy with nonlinear strategic bequests. *European Economic Review, 119*, 548–566.

Canta, C., & Cremer, H. (2021). Opting out and topping up reconsidered: Informal care under uncertain altruism. *Canadian Journal of Economics, 54*(1), 259–283.

Canta, C., Cremer, H., & Gahvari, F. (2020). "Honor thy father and thy mother" or not: Uncertain family aid and the design of social long term care insurance. *Social Choice and Welfare, 55*, 687–734.

Canta, C., Pestieau, P., & Thibault, E. (2016). Long term care and capital accumulation: The impact of the State, the market and the family. *Economic Theory, 61*(4), 755–785.

Cremer, H., & Gahvari, F. (2025). *Endogenous altruism and long term care policies in a Mirrleesian setting*. TSE Working Paper, n 25-1626, mars 2025.

Cremer, H., & Pestieau, P. (1996). Redistributive taxation and social insurance. *International Tax and Public Finance, 3*(3).

Cremer, H. & Roeder, K. (2013). Long-term care policy, myopia and redistribution. *Journal of Public Economics, 108*, 33–43.

Cremer, H. & Roeder, K. (2017). Social insurance with competitive insurance markets and risk misperception. *Journal of Public Economics, 146*, 138–147.

Cremer, H. , Pestieau, P. & Roeder, K. (2016). LTC social insurance with two-sided altruism, *Research in Economics, 70*, 101–109.

Cremer, H., Gahvari, F., & Pestieau, P. (2013). Endogenous altruism, redistribution, and long-term care. *The B.E. Journal of Economic Analysis & Policy, 14*(2), 499–524.

Cremer, H., Klimaviciute, J., & Pestieau, P. (2021). A political economy of loose means-testing in targeted social programs. *Economics Letters, 202*, Article 109810.

Cremer, H., Gahvari, F., & Pestieau, P. (2017). Uncertain altruism and the provision of long term care. *Journal of Public Economics, 151*, 12–24.

Cremer, H., Lozachmeur, J.-M., & Pestieau, P. (2016). The design of long-term care insurance contracts. *Journal of Health Economics, 50*, 330–339.

Cremer, H., & Pestieau, P. (2014). Social long-term care insurance and redistribution. *International Tax and Public Finance, 21*, 955–974.

De Donder, P., & Leroux, M.-L. (2013). Behavioral biases and long-term care insurance: A political economy approach. *The B.E. Journal of Economic Analysis & Policy, 14*, 551–575.

De Donder, P., & Leroux, M.-L. (2017). The political choice of social long term care transfers when family gives time and money. *Social Choice and Welfare, 49*, 755–786.

Diamond, P. A. (1965). National debt in a neoclassical model. *American Economic Review, 55*, 1126–1150.

Drèze, J., Pestieau, P., & Schokkaert, E. (2016). Arrow's theorem of the deductible and long-term care insurance. *Economics Letters, 148*, 103–105.

Drèze, J., & Schokkaert, E. (2013). Arrow's theorem of the deductible: Moral hazard and stop-loss in health insurance. *Journal of Risk and Uncertainty, 47*(2), 147–163.

Jousten, A., Lipszyc, B., Marchand, M., & Pestieau, P. (2005). Long term care insurance and optimal taxation for altruistic children. *FinanzArchiv, 61*, 1–18.

Klimaviciute, J. (2017). Long-term care insurance and intra-family moral hazard: Fixed vs proportional insurance benefits. *The Geneva Risk and Insurance Review, 42*, 87–116.

Klimaviciute, J. (2020). Long-term care and myopic couples. *International Tax and Public Finance, 27*, 77–102.

Klimaviciute, J., & Pestieau, P. (2018). Long-term care social insurance: How to avoid big losses? *International Tax and Public Finance, 25*, 99–139.

Klimaviciute, J., & Pestieau, P. (2018). Social insurance for long-term care with deductible and linear contributions. *FinanzArchiv, 74*, 88–108.

Klimaviciute, J. & Pestieau, P. (2020) Insurance with a deductible. A way out of the long-term care insurance puzzle, *Journal of Economics, 130*, 297–307.

Klimaviciute, J., Perelman, S., Pestieau, P. & Schoenmaeckers, J. (2017). Caring for dependent parents: altruism, exchange or family norm? *Journal of Population Economics, 30*, 835-873.

Lefèbvre, M., Schoenmaeckers, J., & Heymans, L. (2025). Impact of socioeconomic status on loss of autonomy in the old age, unpublished

Leroux, M.-L., & Pestieau, P. (2022). Age-related taxation of bequests in the presence of a dependency risk. *Journal of Public Economic Theory, 24*, 92–119.

Leroux, M.-L., Pestieau, P., & Ponthiere, G. (2021). Fair long-term care insurance. *Social Choice and Welfare, 57*, 503–533.

Lockwood, L. (2018). Incidental bequests and the choice to self-insure late-life risks. *American Economic Review, 108*, 2513–50.

Lozachmeur, J-M., Pestieau, P., & Schoenmackers, J. (2025). Spending down for needs-based LTC programs, unpublished.

Nishimura, Y. & Pestieau, P. (2025) Public pensions and LTC insurance with family solidarity, unpublished.

Nishimura, Y., & Pestieau, P. (2022). Old age or dependence: Which social insurance? *Journal of Public Economic Theory*. https://doi.org/10.1111/jpet.12571

Nuscheler, R., & Roeder, K. (2013). The political economy of long-term care. *European Economic Review, 62*, 154–173.

Pestieau, P. (2026). *The economics of long-term care*. Springer.

Pestieau, P., & Ponthière, G. (2012). The long term care insurance puzzle. In J. Costa-Font & C. Courbage (Eds.), *Financing long term care in Europe: Institutions* (pp. 41–52). Markets and Models: Palgrave Macmillan.

Pestieau, P., & Sato, M. (2008). Long term care: The State, the market and the family. *Economica, 75*, 435–454.

Ponthiere , G., & Thibault, E. (2025). Life time expectancy, income and long-term care. The Preston curve revisited, unpublished.

Rochet, J.-C. (1991). Incentives, redistribution and social insurance. *Geneva Papers on Risk and Insurance Theory, 16*, 143–165.

Samuelson, P. A. (1958). An exact consumption-loan model of interest with or without the social contrivance of money. *Journal of Political Economy, 66*, 467–482.

Chapter 5
Elder Abuse and End of Life

This final chapter departs significantly from its predecessors, examining two critical issues that define life's final stages and pose fundamentally ethical rather than economic questions. The first explores the vulnerability of frail elderly individuals to mistreatment during their most defenseless period. The second investigates how policymakers might best structure end-of-life care frameworks.

5.1 Elder Abuse in Vulnerable Populations

The shadow of abuse looms darkly over many of our most vulnerable elderly citizens. This crisis—encompassing physical violence, emotional cruelty, sexual exploitation, financial predation, and callous neglect—strikes at the heart of our social contract to protect those who can no longer fully protect themselves. Frailty renders many elderly individuals particularly defenseless, their physical limitations, and cognitive decline creating a perfect storm of dependency. According to comprehensive research published in The Lancet Global Health,[1] the statistics paint a disturbing portrait: nearly 16% of people aged 60 and older have suffered at the hands of those meant to care for them. This research—drawing from 52 studies across 28 countries—reveals a troubling pattern: 11.6% endured psychological abuse, 6.8% suffered financial exploitation, 4.2% experienced neglect, 2.6% faced physical violence, and 0.9% were victims of sexual abuse. Even vigilant family members often miss the telltale indicators of abuse, which manifest in various concerning ways. Physical signs appear as unexplained injuries, untreated medical conditions, or suspicious bruising patterns. Emotional markers emerge through withdrawal, depression, unusual fearfulness, or sudden anxiety. Financial exploitation reveals itself in mysterious account changes, missing valuables, or unauthorized transactions. Neglect becomes evident in unsafe

[1] https://www.thelancet.com/journals/langlo/article/PIIS2214-109X(17)30006-2/fulltext.

P. Pestieau, *The Economics of Long-term Care*, Developments in Health Economics and Public Policy 14, https://doi.org/10.1007/978-3-032-18237-1_5

living environments, inadequate nutrition, inappropriate clothing, or untreated medical issues like bedsores. The problem extends beyond individual cases to systemic failures. In France, Vincent Castanet's explosive expos triggered nationwide outrage by documenting how profit-driven care facilities routinely sacrifice resident dignity for financial gain.[2] This scandal forced political leaders to confront the urgent need for nursing home reform.

A Michigan study[3] revealed the shocking prevalence of staff-perpetrated abuse, with nearly one-quarter of nursing home residents reporting at least one incident of physical violence from caregivers. This research identified key risk factors: limitations in activities of daily living, behavioral challenges, and previous victimization all significantly increased abuse likelihood. While these studies focus primarily on institutional settings, family-based elder abuse remains distressingly common. We can identify factors contributing to abuse; however, nothing justifies mistreatment of vulnerable elders. The institutional failures stem largely from chronic understaffing and inadequate training—problems especially acute in private facilities where profit motives drive aggressive cost-cutting. In America, many unqualified nursing assistants earn more at fast-food establishments than caring for our elderly. Better compensation, benefits, and training would bring dignity to this essential work while reducing abuse incidents[4]

Though profit-seeking often bears blame, Dewatripont (2023) proposes transforming listed companies into "mission companies"—legal structures balancing shareholder interests with those of residents and staff. However, elder abuse pervades non-profit facilities and family settings as well, suggesting deeper underlying issues. Domestic abuse frequently results from the toxic combination of heavy dependency and inadequate living conditions. Yet even with improved staffing and family support, certain difficult scenarios would persist. Two particularly challenging situations defy easy solutions: First, cases where dependent individuals display consistently malicious behavior testing even the most patient caregiver's limits. Second, the common scenario where dementia combined with incontinence creates overwhelming caregiving demands. Home care in these situations carries extreme risks, potentially destroying caregivers' physical and mental health. Institutionalization becomes necessary, but requires sufficient qualified staff to manage these exhausting cases.

One partial answer may lie in robotic assistance technologies, which offer the significant advantage of never experiencing frustration or exasperation—much like a GPS system remaining perpetually calm despite repeated user errors. Truly addressing elder abuse demands vigilance, education, and proactive engagement from caregivers, families, and communities alike. By recognizing warning signs early and implementing preventative measures systematically, we can better protect our elderly from harm while ensuring they receive the respect and dignified care they deserve.

---

[2] Castanet (2022).

[3] https://www.michigan.gov/ag/initiatives/elder-abuse.

[4] https://nap.nationalacademies.org/catalog/26526/the-national-imperative-to-improve-nursing-home-quality-honoring-our.

The role of assistive technologies isn't substitution but intelligent complementation. Technologies can handle routine, repetitive, and monitoring tasks, freeing caregivers to focus on the irreplaceable human elements—emotional connection, complex decision-making, and meaningful interaction. Sensors, wearable devices, and smart home systems can continuously track vital signs, detect falls, monitor medication adherence, and identify changes in daily routines that might signal health issues. This augments what a caregiver can observe during limited visits and enables earlier intervention. A caregiver visiting twice daily can effectively "extend" their presence through these systems. Exoskeletons and robotic lifting devices can reduce the enormous physical strain on caregivers, preventing injuries that force people out of care work. Transfer assists, mobility aids with AI navigation, and even more advanced robots that help with dressing or bathing could emerge. These don't replace the caregiver but make their work sustainable. For individuals with dementia or cognitive decline, technologies like medication reminders, GPS tracking for wandering prevention, interactive memory aids, and even social robots that provide companionship and cognitive stimulation can fill gaps between caregiver visits. Some studies suggest social robots reduce loneliness and agitation.[5]

5.2 End of Life[6]

The twilight of human existence—that delicate transition we call the end of life—demands our deepest attention when examining disability and dependence in old age. Death might arrive suddenly like a thief in the night, or it may announce itself through a prolonged procession of decline and suffering. Across the globe, societies have crafted vastly different approaches to this universal passage, each reflecting cultural values, economic realities, and ethical frameworks. The modern challenge lies in finding the optimal balance between state involvement, market mechanisms, and family responsibility during life's final chapter. Our current medical paradigm often defaults to aggressive interventions, extending life at any cost. Yet a compelling case emerges for redirecting our focus toward comprehensive palliative care—an approach that promises to reduce social insurance burdens, lighten families' financial loads, and most crucially, spare patients from unnecessary suffering during their final days.

The very concept of planning for life's end is relatively new in human history. Merely a century ago, discussions about pension systems rarely entered public discourse, as average life expectancy hovered below 65 years. The demographic reality meant few individuals lived long enough to require extended retirement support. As longevity increased, however, pension policy quickly ascended to the forefront of social priorities. This dramatic shift in lifespan simultaneously triggered a cascade of age-related disabilities, forcing societies to confront questions of dependency and

[5] See, e.g., Lee et al. (2025) and Pu et al. (2019).

[6] This section is based on Perelman and Pestieau (2024).

diminished autonomy through long-term care initiatives. More recently, attention has shifted toward end-of-life concerns—a term that resists simple definition. When precisely does this final phase begin? For the young adult tragically lost in a highway collision, the end arrives in an instant. Many healthcare systems consider this phase initiated when recovery hopes vanish, triggering specialized care protocols often accompanied by extraordinarily generous reimbursement structures.

5.2.1 *Medicalization of End-of-Life Care*

The end-of-life period begins at the point at which there can be no further recovery or cure, and the only way out is death. During this period, there should be a change in the type of healthcare provided. Most healthcare systems and traditional medical approaches focus on curative interventions. While curative care aims to improve and prolong quality of life, not all illnesses are curable. Curative interventions for incurable diseases may not prolong life or improve its quality. What's more, they are often costly for individuals, their families, and healthcare systems as a whole. These healthcare systems are focused on healing, and tend to keep patients alive, even at the cost of pain, suffering and a deterioration in their quality of life, regardless of the expected success of the care. Preparing or planning for death remains outside the normal care process, leaving people with terminal illnesses with limited opportunity to choose the level of medical intervention they prefer. So, instead of focusing on intensive procedures with little clinical benefit and no improvement in quality of life, some research is now concentrating on the "quality of death." This section compares the quality of palliative care in different countries.

The period preceding admission to palliative care is sometimes a time when family and doctors may be tempted, for different reasons, to prolong life, sometimes at the price of unbearable suffering for the patient and high costs for families. Many people, especially at advanced ages, wish to avoid therapeutic overkill. This is not always possible, for two reasons. Firstly, the dividing line between aggressive therapy and palliative care is not always clear. Secondly, some doctors, more so in a country like the USA than in Belgium or the Netherlands, take the Hippocratic oath to the letter. As this oath says, " I will not administer a poison to anybody when asked to do so, nor will I suggest such a course." As a result, many doctors are unwilling to resign themselves to their patient's death through assisted suicide, as long as there is hope of keeping him or her alive. It is in the name of this oath that they are reluctant, even opposed, to euthanizing their patient, even where this is perfectly legal and despite the patient's wishes.

In broad terms, palliative care is any treatment or intervention intended to control pain or other distressing symptoms. Palliative care can be provided in an institution such as a hospice or outside of hospice. In hospice, palliative care aims to relieve suffering by managing physical symptoms such as nausea, shortness of breath, and constipation that may be caused by the illness or result from side effects of medication. Hospice-based palliative care also addresses other issues such as anxiety, insomnia, or depression. Some hospices offer complementary therapies such as healing touch, meditation, aroma therapy, music therapy, and pet therapy. Non-denominational, non-judgmental hospice chaplains offer an opportunity for spiritual exploration and discussion.

Palliative care outside of hospice may be used during any point in the illness. Patients may receive palliative care while they receive treatment aimed at curing or slowing the progression of their disease. Sometimes such treatments (e.g., chemotherapy, radiation, etc.) can be better tolerated with the help of palliative care, making it a good option for people who are not in the final stages of illness but who desire expert pain and symptom management.

5.2.2 *The Costs*

It is important to note that the costs of end-of-life care can be influenced by factors such as the availability of palliative care services, the prevalence of advance care planning and the use of aggressive medical interventions. The USA often has higher end-of-life care costs than many other developed countries. This is partly due to the widespread use of aggressive medical interventions, a fee-for-service healthcare system and a cultural tendency to pursue life-prolonging treatments. In contrast, European countries such as the Netherlands and Belgium have well-established palliative care programs. In these countries, end-of-life care may focus more on improving patients' quality of life than on aggressive medical interventions. That said, there are variations between countries in terms of their stance on the issue of end-of-life care. The example of Canada is interesting. Here, the healthcare system is publicly funded, and it takes several months to get most medical appointments. However, as soon as a patient is declared to be EOL (end of life), these barriers come down. They have the right to unrestricted end-of-life care. This care can be provided on the premises of a palliative care home or at home. This contrast between limited access to health care before the end of life and unrestricted access after the patient is deemed to be at the end of life is found to a greater or lesser extent in most countries. The reasons for this difference in treatment are open to question. Could it be a way for the state to compensate individuals for their impending death? Even if the out-of-pocket expenses can be substantial, health care at the end of life is for the most part covered by social insurance. Clearly, the decision to enter palliative care remains the responsibility of the patient and his or her family. However, this decision has a definitive budgetary impact. A recent study[7] conducted in Canada shows that increased use of palliative care services should lead to a reduction in end-of-life costs.

---

[7] Cost-effectiveness of palliative care (2022) https://www.acsp.net/wp-content/uploads/2024/01/TWF-Cost-Effectiveness-Document-de-travail-FR.

5.2.3 The Family

The quality of end-of-life care, whether at home or in an institution, often depends on the family circle. The family plays a decisive and, more often than not, positive role. Being surrounded by loved ones is comforting. The end of life is undoubtedly the time of life when people feel most vulnerable and fragile. To be able to count on the loving, selfless assistance of loved ones to protect them is essential, especially in the case of mental degeneration. The family can protect the individual from herself (falls, injuries...) or from others (abuse of weakness), but care must be taken not to go too far and to respect the patient's principle of self-determination. This means respecting their ability to decide for themselves, and to be free to make their own choices for as long as possible. Being old doesn't mean being incompetent or a sub-citizen, especially when you still have all your wits about you. And even with cognitive diseases such as Alzheimer's, it's perfectly possible to continue to make one's own choices up to an advanced stage. Unfortunately, this is not guaranteed.

A troubling paradox emerges when children genuinely believe they're acting in their parent's best interest—investing enormous energy and making real sacrifices—while simultaneously undermining the very person they're trying to help. They override expressed preferences, impose their own vision of care without truly listening, use their role to maintain control or fulfill unexamined psychological needs, and become so consumed by physical tasks that emotional needs and dignity fall away. The paradox deepens because these caregivers often work themselves to exhaustion. Their sacrifice is real, which makes it nearly impossible for them to hear that they might be causing harm. They can genuinely love their parent while simultaneously mistreating them—not through malice, but through a kind of suffocating devotion. This pattern might be called well-intentioned harm or benevolent overreach.

Take the following scenario of an old person at the end of her life. She would have so much liked her suffering to have been shortened by a dignified euthanasia. This was refused by a reluctant family and an obtuse doctor taking advantage of her weakened state. Before that, when she still had a good part of her head, she was subjected to benevolent overreach. Her children put her in a shabby nursing home she didn't want, for her own good of course. Still, for her own good, they put her under guardianship, so that she no longer has any control over her income and assets.

How do you avoid such hell? It's not easy. Even more complicated than avoiding institutional abuse, or even cynical family abuse. In this case, the abuser is convinced of his right to do so. He behaves in this way for the good of the dependent person, who doesn't know what's good for her. Added to this is the fact that, in extreme cases, the legal system always sides with the family. It's clear that once set in motion, this infernal scenario cannot be stopped. So, we need to prevent and anticipate. The best way to prevent this is undoubtedly to invest emotionally in the family. In Asian countries, for example, there has been a change in the way children are brought up. Parents are gradually abandoning the strict style of what is known as "tiger parenting"[8] for a style imbued with patience and love, which takes longer but ensures that they can count on their children in their old age in case of need.[9]

That said, even with the best will in the world, it's not always possible to avoid such altruistic abuse, and it's important to take action long before it's too late. The situation varies widely from country to country. The proportion of elderly people who have a written plan designating a person who will make decisions about their treatment ranges from 67% in the USA and 62% in Canada to 16% in the Netherlands.[10] These are elementary precautions which, in most cases, will be of no use, as the majority of end-of-life situations are, fortunately, more harmonious than those just described.

5.2.4 *The Legal and Cultural Dimensions of End-of-Life Care: A Global Perspective*

End-of-life legislation varies dramatically across national boundaries, creating a complex global patchwork of approaches to life's final chapter. While no jurisdiction explicitly prohibits aggressive medical intervention—and some healthcare systems tacitly encourage such approach—the legal frameworks governing euthanasia and assisted dying reveal profound cultural and ethical differences worldwide. The Netherlands and Belgium stand at the progressive edge of this spectrum, permitting euthanasia under stringent conditions that require both the patient's explicit request and evidence of unbearable suffering. Switzerland has carved out its own distinctive approach, legalizing assisted suicide in specific circumstances, with organizations like Dignitas and Exit providing these services to individuals with terminal illnesses. Canada's system of Medical Assistance in Dying (MAD) operates under precise eligibility requirements, including the presence of a serious, irremediable medical condition, while carefully distinguishing between active and passive forms of euthanasia[11] According to a recent comprehensive survey,[12] active euthanasia—where medical professionals directly administer life-ending medication—remains legal in only eight jurisdictions globally: Australia, Belgium, Canada, Colombia, Luxembourg, the Netherlands, New Zealand, and Spain. The more conservative approach of passive euthanasia—withdrawing life-sustaining treatment rather than

---

[8] Tiger parenting is a style of parenting that emphasizes academic achievement, life success, and discipline. Tiger parents are strict and stress the importance of school performance and career development, often by setting high expectations and withholding affection.

[9] See on this Fan et al. (2025).

[10] American Academy of Actuaries (2017), End-of-Life Care in an Aging World: A Global Perspective https://www.actuary.org/endoflifecare#:~:text= Issues%20surrounding%20end%2Dof%2Dlife,economic%20burdens%20on%20future%20generations.

[11] Active euthanasia: killing a patient by active means, for example, injecting a patient with a lethal dose of a drug. Sometimes called "aggressive" euthanasia. Passive euthanasia: intentionally letting a patient die by withholding artificial life support such as a ventilator or feeding tube.

[12] World Population Review (2023) https://worldpopulationreview.com/country-rankings/where-is-euthanasialegal.

actively intervening—enjoys broader acceptance, permitted in Argentina, Chile, Finland, Germany, India, Ireland, Japan, Mexico, Portugal, South Korea, Sweden, Switzerland, the UK, and several states in the USA. This landscape continues to evolve rapidly as more nations contemplate legalizing various forms of assisted dying. In France, while assisted dying remains prohibited, vigorous public discourse and legislative efforts signal potential change on the horizon. Notably, in jurisdictions where these practices have been legalized, utilization rates have not surged dramatically, contradicting the dire predictions of opponents.

The availability of euthanasia offers patients a crucial psychological safety net—the reassurance that excessive suffering can be avoided—even when this option ultimately goes unexercised. At this point, one could also bring up the increasingly popular concept of the death doula. A death doula, also known as a death midwife, is a non-medical professional who provides support to individuals and their families during the dying process. They offer emotional, spiritual, and practical support, helping individuals navigate the end-of-life journey with dignity and peace.

This matter naturally intersects with broader discussions on suicide, which disproportionately affects elderly populations in most countries, despite being the leading cause of death among younger demographics. These statistics likely underrepresent the true scope of elder suicide, and anecdotal evidence suggests that informal end-of-life assistance from primary care physicians occurs more frequently than official records indicate. Research has not demonstrated that euthanasia access reduces suicide rates in the general population.

The striking variations in end-of-life care approaches across different societies reflect deep-seated cultural, religious, and societal differences. These distinctions manifest not only in legal attitudes toward assisted dying but also in the structure and accessibility of palliative care services. The same cultural factors shape how different societies honor patient autonomy and self-determination in end-of-life decision-making.

In countries like France, the geographic distribution of palliative care facilities reveals troubling regional disparities, creating fundamental inequities in service accessibility. This uneven landscape produces cascading consequences, with vulnerable populations facing disproportionate barriers to essential end-of-life services. The stark reality is that socioeconomic status profoundly influences end-of-life care quality and options, amplifying broader patterns of inequality at life's most vulnerable moment.

5.2.5 *Japan and Its Old People*

Japan holds a stark distinction in the demography of aging: exceptionally low fertility paired with some of the world's longest lifespans. The consequences are staggering. The nation's current population of 128 million is projected to contract to 87 million by 2060 and just 51 million by 2100. By century's end, nearly 40% of Japanese will be over 65. Meanwhile, public debt has reached alarming levels, and the effective retirement age hovers near 70. Yet even with people working into their late sixties, the country struggles to sustain its pay-as-you-go pension system. Younger generations increasingly feel trapped in an intergenerational squeeze. In a country where euthanasia remains illegal, this demographic crisis has sparked some disturbing responses. Yusuke Narita, a young economist teaching at Yale University, has gained attention by addressing what he calls the "burden" of Japan's aging society. In recent public appearances,[13] he stated bluntly: "I have the impression that the only solution is quite clear. In the end, isn't it mass suicide and mass 'seppuku'[14] of the elderly?" Though thankfully still a minority view, this sentiment has prompted artistic pushback. Japanese filmmaker Chie Hayakawa recently released "Plan 75," a dystopian film featuring cheerful salespeople who encourage pensioners to accept government-sponsored euthanasia. Hayakawa's aim was to expose the dangerous extremes of gerontophobia—to show where such thinking inevitably leads. Here, an important distinction must be made. The current challenge of pension financing, while serious, can be addressed through policy without resorting to such barbarism. This differs fundamentally from the circumstances of primitive societies where genuine resource scarcity meant that the elderly surviving too long could threaten the group's survival. Such ancient practices echo through Japanese folklore, where families would abandon their aged parents on remote mountaintops or in forest clearings to die. This dark tradition inspired the 1958 film "The Ballad of Narayama" and its 1983 remake—both, like "Plan 75," recognized at Cannes. Rejecting extreme solutions doesn't mean inaction. Japan has other levers at its disposal: immigration reform, pro-natalist policies, and adjustments to retirement age. The country simply needs the will to pull them.

5.2.6 Patient Participation

Determining the exact amount of costs incurred by patients for end-of-life treatments can be difficult, as it depends on a variety of factors, including the healthcare system, insurance coverage, individual treatment choices, and the availability of support services. In addition, cultural and societal factors can influence the preferences and choices of patients and their families at the end of life. The overall cost of end-of-life treatments can vary considerably, depending on factors such as the country or region, the specific medical interventions required, and the healthcare system in place. End-of-life treatments can include palliative care, medications, medical procedures, and other supportive care. In many countries, end-of-life care is covered by health insurance or state-funded healthcare systems, which can help ease the financial burden on individuals and their families. However, out-of-pocket expenses

[13] https://www.nytimes.com/2023/02/12/world/asia/japan-elderly-mass-suicide.html?searchResultPosition.

[14] Seppuku is a form of taking one's own life that was considered honourable among the feudal Japanese samurai class.

may still arise for a variety of reasons, including co-payments, uncovered services, and certain medications. In some regions where access to healthcare is limited or insurance coverage inadequate, individuals and families may bear a greater financial burden for end-of-life treatments. The result can be significant disparities in access to quality care, and financial strain for families who are already coping with the emotional challenges of end-of-life situations. It is essential to bear in mind that data on the overall costs of end-of-life treatments may not be readily available or accurately documented due to variations in healthcare systems, reporting practices and cultural differences. In most countries, the palliative care phase, whether at home or in an institution, is fully reimbursed by social insurance. However, before this phase, when families and patients are tempted to undergo interventions, whose sole aim is to prolong life by a few weeks, the out-of-pocket expenses can be considerable. In other words, the relentless pursuit of treatment leads to suffering and expense.

5.2.7 Where to Die?

Using data from the European SHARE survey, Orlovic et al.(2017) attempt to compare where people die in around 20 countries, i.e., at home, in a nursing home or in hospital, with the implication that the latter solution is the costliest for families. They show that the increased use of ambulatory long-term care facilities in countries with higher public spending on long-term care leads to a reduction in hospital admissions and an increase in the proportion of out-of-hospital deaths, compared with countries where end-of-life care is mainly privately financed, which tend to have underdeveloped and underused formal long-term care facilities. As a result, end-of-life care in privately-funded countries is more hospital-based. Focusing on Belgium, Gielen et al. (2010) show that life ending in hospitals is more expensive than in palliative care centers.

Figure 5.1 shows places of death in a sample of European countries using SHARE updated data. This figure shows that the fraction of people who are in a nursing home or hospice at the time of death is particularly high in Sweden, Switzerland, the Netherlands, and Denmark, which are known to have particularly high levels of public LTC insurance. In these same countries, the proportion of people dying in hospital is relatively low. Of course, age and cause of death—cancer, heart disease, respiratory problems or other—are related and can influence the place of death.

At the time of death, there are some people who suffer no dependency at all, and who are perfectly autonomous. However, they represent a minority, as Fig. 5.2 shows. Portugal is the country where people have the most physical or cognitive problems, and Greece has the least, followed by Austria and Switzerland. In terms of disabilities, we distinguish between limitations in the exercise of daily activities (ADL) and cognitive dependencies, separate and combined.

It is also interesting to compare countries according to the time spent by individuals in an institution of any kind in the last year of life. According to Fig. 5.3, France is the country where most people spend the whole of their last year of life at home.

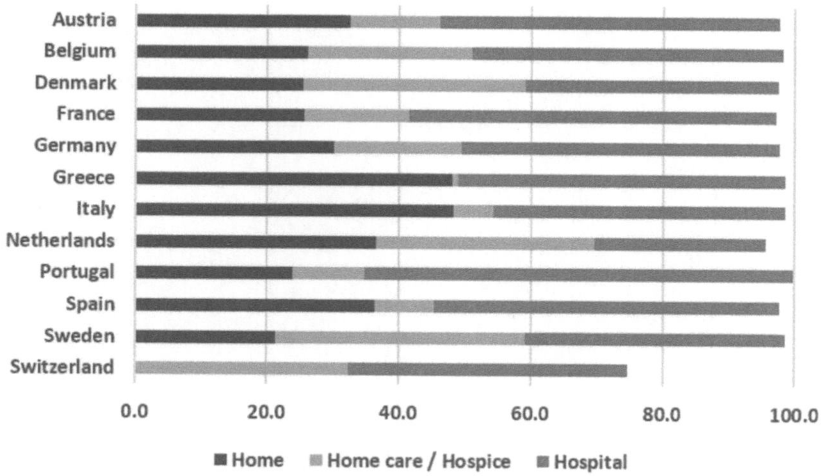

Fig. 5.1 Place of death in Europe (in %) *Source* SHARE Survey. Own calculations based on information reported by relatives of the deceased respondent (Waves 2–8, 2005–2020)

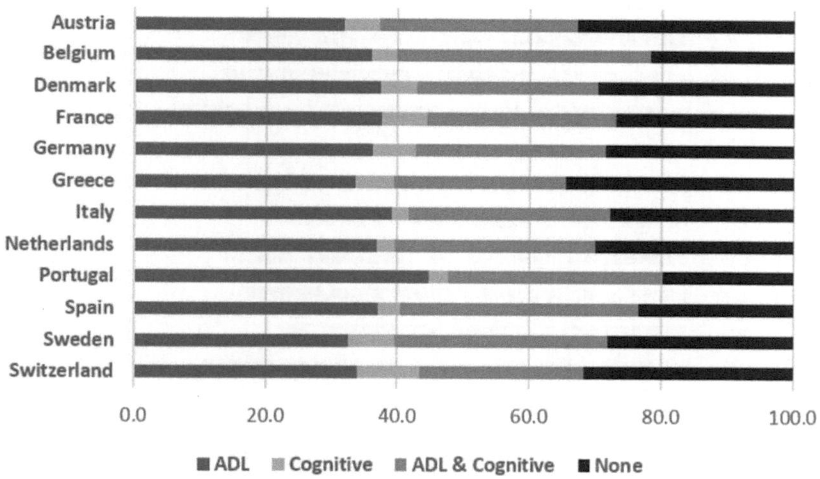

Fig. 5.2 Type of dependency in the last year of life (in %). *Source* See Fig. 5.1

More generally, this trend is found in southern European countries. To the contrary, in Sweden and generally northern European countries, people are the most likely to spend the last year of their lives in an institution. In Europe, the use of palliative care varies greatly from country to country. Figure 5.4 shows data for a sample of countries, with variations ranging from 18% in Austria to 52% in Greece for people dying over the age of 64. This figure includes palliative care received at home, in nursing home, in hospital, and in specialized centers.

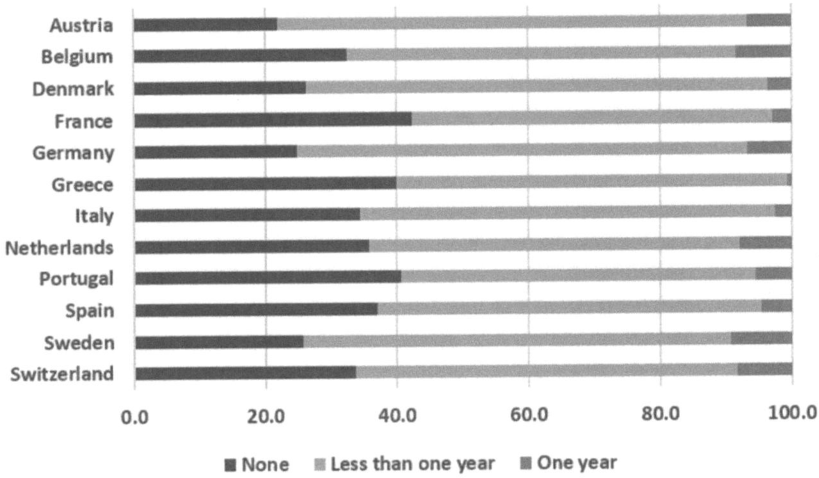

Fig. 5.3 Time spent in an institution during the last year of life (in %). *Source* See Fig. 5.1

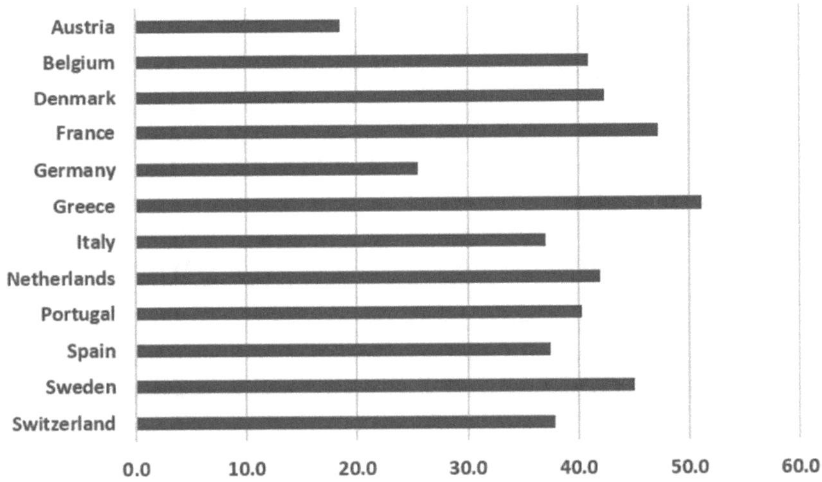

Fig. 5.4 Share of people who used palliative care before dying (aged 65 or over). *Source* SHARE Survey, Waves 7 and 8 (2017–2020)

5.2.8 Need of Reorientation

Among all stages of life, the final phase is marked by heightened vulnerability, both physically and emotionally. As individuals approach the end of life, the need for tranquility and peace becomes paramount. However, numerous obstacles can hinder this pursuit, including the indifference or self-interest of relatives and friends, a medical system more focused on cure than comfort, inadequate social support, and legal frameworks that fail to fully uphold the dignity of dying individuals. Addressing these challenges requires a legislative and social support system that prioritizes the wishes of patients regarding crucial end-of-life decisions. These include managing personal assets, choosing where to spend one's final days, deciding between palliative care and euthanasia, or refusing aggressive medical interventions.

While some countries have made progress in these areas, much remains to be done to ensure that every individual can end their life freely and with dignity. Beyond the moral considerations, practical concerns also arise, particularly regarding the growing financial burden of end-of-life care on both the state and individual families. The suffering associated with this stage is often profound, making it imperative to shift toward greater investment in palliative care and a reassessment of conventional treatment approaches that frequently result in excessive and futile medical interventions. Such a shift would bring multiple benefits: reducing pressure on social security systems, alleviating financial strain on families, and most importantly, preventing unnecessary suffering. Moving toward a patient-centered, dignity-affirming approach to end-of-life care is not only a compassionate choice but also a socially and economically responsible one.

References

Castanet, V. (2022). *Les Fossoyeurs*. Grasset.

Dewatripont, M. (2023). Quel statut juridique et quelles missions pour des EHPAD visage humain?, Revue d" conomie financi re, no 152.

Fan, S., Pang, Y., & Pestieau, P. (2025). The intriguing relation between parenting styles and eldercare. *Review of Economics of the Household: Decision*. (forthcoming).

Gielen, B., Remacle, A., & Mertens, R. (2010). Patterns of health care use and expenditure during the last 6 months of life in Belgium: Differences between age categories in cancer and non-cancer patients. *Health Policy, 97*, 53–61

Lee, S. H., Kim, J. S., & Yu, S. (2025). The impact of care robots on older adults: A systematic review. *Journal of Advanced Nursing* (published online July 15, 2025).

Orlovic, M., Marti, J., & Mossialos, E. (2017). Analysis of end-of-life care, out-of-pocket spending, and place of death in 16 European countries and Israel. *Health Affairs, 36*. https://www.healthaffairs.org/doi/10.1377/hlthaff.2017.0166

Perelman, S., & Pestieau, P. (2024). How to Manage the End of Life. *An International Perspective, Journal of Palliative and Medical Care, 3*, 101.

Pu, L., Moyle, W., Jones, C., & Todorovic, M. (2019). The effectiveness of social robots for older adults: A systematic review and meta-analysis of randomized controlled studies. *The Gerontologist, 59*(1), e37–e51.

Chapter 6
Conclusion

In the twilight of his life, Baumgartner[1], the protagonist of Paul Auster's last novel, reflects on the future that still lies ahead. "Time matters now, and he has no idea how much of it remains. Not just how many years until he 'kicks the bucket,' but more precisely, how many years of active, productive life he has left before his mind or body—or both—begin to fail him, turning him into an incompetent fool, wracked with pain, unable to read or think, unable to remember what was said four seconds ago, or summon enough energy to have sex—a horrible thought he does not wish to entertain. Five years? Ten years? Fifteen? The days and months now race past him more quickly, and the time he has left will pass, in any case, in the blink of an eye." This uncertainty is one of the differences between youth and old age. One can clearly distinguish childhood from adolescence. However, the duration of the two stages of old age—one of good health and autonomy, the other of dependency and various impairments—remains uncertain. It's true that, on average, in a given country and at a certain time, from the age of 65, the first stage lasts around 10 years, and the second about 8 years. But these are merely statistical averages. On an individual level, the length of old age and the distribution between these two stages can vary enormously.

Some may lose all autonomy at 65 and live only a few more years, while others remain independent for decades, experiencing only a short period of dependency. According to this binary perspective, during the first phase, individuals retain both physical and mental health, maintain a high level of independence, and actively engage in social, recreational, and possibly even professional activities. They face only minor or no health issues, managing them effectively with regular check-ups and a healthy lifestyle. They often continue exercising, eat a balanced diet, and sustain a strong social network. They still enjoy hobbies, travel, volunteer, and participate in family commitments, while their cognitive functions remain sharp. The second phase is characterized by significant health problems, declining physical and cognitive abilities, and increased dependence on others for daily activities and care. Chronic

[1] Auster (2023).

P. Pestieau, *The Economics of Long-term Care*, Developments in Health Economics and Public Policy 14, https://doi.org/10.1007/978-3-032-18237-1_6

diseases, mobility issues, and cognitive decline (such as dementia) become more common. The elderly may have frequent medical appointments, hospitalizations, and require continuous medication management. Their participation in previous leisure and social activities may drastically decrease. Significant support is needed, ranging from help with daily activities (bathing, dressing, eating) to full-time care. This support might come from family members, professional caregivers, or assisted living facilities. In general, the transition from one phase to the other is not abrupt. Most often, unless there is a sudden event like a stroke, the shift is gradual. Physical and cognitive decline can be slow, almost imperceptible.

There are scales, such as the widely used Katz Index, that help assess a person's level of dependence and thus determine whether they have entered the second stage of old age. It is important to note that while we can recognize when an elderly person shifts into heavy dependence, we cannot predict when they might transition from a state of well-being to one of unhappiness. It is clear that in the first phase of old age, there is little need for LTC. On the contrary, by helping their children in caring for their grandchildren, elderly people can create favorable conditions for care the day they lose autonomy. The second phase is the period that will need attention. In this work, we have demonstrated that the demand for long-term care (LTC) will continue to rise in the coming decades. To meet this growing need, both family and the market will be crucial. The family appears to play a less significant role than it did in the past, and the market remains conspicuously absent. This leaves the state as the key actor. In the future, its involvement will need to increase. We have presented a series of ideas and proposals aimed at developing a comprehensive social insurance system to cover the loss of autonomy in the elderly. It is indeed possible to address this rapid increase in LTC demand, but doing so requires genuine political will.

As a final comment, let me address a growing concern shared by many. Most countries have traditionally met the needs of disabled elderly individuals by relying heavily on younger generations' contributions. However, with populations rapidly aging, this intergenerational arrangement faces mounting pressure. The declining ratio of working-age individuals to retirees raises serious questions about the long-term viability of this model. If younger generations—already challenged by rising costs, stagnant wages, and economic uncertainty—become overwhelmed, they may resist further contributions, creating political and financial strain on welfare systems. In such circumstances, there exists a genuine risk that governments, struggling to balance competing demands, may begin neglecting the frail elderly. Budget constraints could lead to reduced long-term care funding, more restrictive eligibility requirements, or an increasing shift of responsibilities to families who may lack the resources or capacity to provide adequate support. Without proactive policy adjustments—such as diversifying funding sources, promoting private savings, or implementing efficiency-driven reforms—this model may become unsustainable, leaving vulnerable populations at risk of inadequate care. Let us hope that the alarming prospect of societies abandoning their most vulnerable members remains a warning rather than becoming our reality.

Reference

Auster, P. (2023). *Baumgartner*. NYC: Grove.

MIX
Papier aus verantwortungsvollen Quellen
Paper from responsible sources
FSC® C105338

If you have any concerns about our products,
you can contact us on
ProductSafety@springernature.com

In case Publisher is established outside the EU,
the EU authorized representative is:
Springer Nature Customer Service Center GmbH
Europaplatz 3, 69115 Heidelberg, Germany

Printed by Libri Plureos GmbH
in Hamburg, Germany